BREE GRINNED AT HIM LIKE A MISCHIEVOUS ELF. "YOU'RE not the only one who can tease around here, mister. I may have taken my major in practical stuff like computers and business at school, but I took drama for fun."

That was it. Cody wouldn't be tricked this many times in one day. He sat down and pulled Bree onto his lap. She shrieked in laughter and landed on top of him. It would have been a great move if he hadn't been in an office chair with wheels. The chair threatened to dump both of them as Bree struggled to get her balance.

She smelled so good. A little bit of sea breeze mixed with a delicate floral perfume. The scent was as elusive as the woman herself. Cody slid one hand around the back of her neck, gently pulling her down to meet him. "Come here." The husky rasp of his voice surprised him.

Bree obeyed. Wide eyes fringed with impossibly long, dark lashes swam into focus directly in front of his face. "I'm here," she said softly. "What do you want, Cody?"

"More than I can have. More than I'll take."

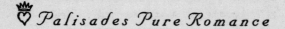
Palisades Pure Romance

Island Breeze

LYNN BULOCK

Palisades is a division of Multnomah Publishers, Inc.

ISLAND BREEZE
published by Palisades
a division of Multnomah Publishers, Inc.

© 1999 by Lynn Bulock
International Standard Book Number: 1-57673-398-X

Design by Andrea Gjeldum
Cover image of palm trees by Photodisc
Cover background by Digital Stock

Scripture quotations are from:
The Holy Bible, New International Version © 1973, 1984 by International Bible
Society, used by permission of Zondervan Publishing House

Palisades is a trademark of Multnomah Publishers, Inc., and is registered in the
U.S. Patent and Trademark Office.

Printed in the United States of America

For information:
MULTNOMAH PUBLISHERS, INC.•P.O. BOX 1720•SISTERS, OREGON 97759
Library of Congress Cataloging-in-Publication Data
Bulock, Lynn.   Island breeze   p. cm.   ISBN 1-57673-398-X (alk. paper)
PS3552.U463i85   1999   98–27819   813'.54—dc21   CIP

OPM   99 00 01 02 03 04 05 — 10 9 8 7 6 5 4 3 2 1

To Joe, always.
And in loving memory of
Lt. James Joseph Cacciabando Sr.

For God did not give us a spirit of timidity,
but a spirit of power,
of love and of self-discipline.

2 TIMOTHY 1:7

Prologue

FUNNY, HE DIDN'T LOOK LIKE A MONSTER. BREE TREHEARN gazed into Bo's eyes, and the same sullen, heavyset man she'd known before looked back at her. His computer sat on the counter between them at BiTs & Pieces, and he was waving a copy of her latest coupon from the Yorktown *Banner*.

"I would have given you the special price anyway, Bo." Bree finally made her voice work. She had to act normal, even though Bo terrified her now—now that she knew what she did.

"You're too kind, Bree." Yesterday he had been only quiet. Today his soft voice sounded threatening. Bree's whole perspective of the man had changed, and she couldn't go back again.

She still wanted to confront him with what she had

found on his computer. The lists she'd stumbled upon while looking for the problem on his hard drive shocked and horrified her. So many conflicting emotions were at work in her: fear, anger, hope that she could say the right words to what was obviously a troubled soul.

"So you took care of everything?" His pale eyes behind the thick glasses seemed suspicious. "No problems?"

"No problems." Bree willed her hands not to shake. She knew the right thing to do would be to confront him now, but she couldn't do it. "Your operation speed should increase dramatically."

"Great. Worth every penny." Bo pulled out his battered wallet and paid her in twenty-dollar bills.

She gave him change—and hesitated. Now was her chance to do the right thing. She should confront Bo with what she'd found on his hard drive in those cache files he probably didn't know existed. She should tell him she was calling the police and giving them the information she'd stored on a disk in the shop. But she didn't. She couldn't. Fear held her silent. Instead she watched him pick up the computer case and walk out to his car.

When he was gone, Bree slumped against the counter. "What a coward I am." She knew that doing the right thing in this situation meant calling the police and telling them what Bo was doing with his computer.

That didn't feel right when she had been praying for him, witnessing to him both vocally and by example. She shook her head. She would take another course of action—and pray she was doing the right thing.

She was banking on the hope that if Bo had brought her the machine for service in the first place, he didn't know enough about it to realize what she'd done. The first time Bo tried to access those lists and documents, either to change one of them or print one out, his hard drive was going to crash. It would appear that everything was wiped out, permanently. If Bree was right about his computer expertise or lack of it, Bo would blame himself for the problem. He'd never know she had copied his information then rigged the original to destroy itself.

Of course, if she was wrong, she would know very soon. Bree prayed that she wasn't wrong.

It didn't take long to find out otherwise. The hang-up phone calls started at midnight. Near morning the caller started speaking in a harsh, threatening voice hardly recognizable as Bo's. "I know what you did, Bree," the caller rasped. "And it was stupid. Very, very stupid. I abhor stupidity."

Bree hung up the phone hard, too shocked to say

anything. Her hands shook so that she could barely put the handset in the cradle. With each call the threats got uglier. By dawn Bree disconnected the phone.

A truck cruised slowly by her house shortly after daylight. Panicked now, Bree's only response was flight. It was too late to try to put this whole mess to rights.

An hour later she was on the road, everything of value to her stuffed in her little car. There wasn't much that she truly valued, not that belonged to her. She made sure that everyone whose computers she still had for maintenance or repair got them back or knew to come get them free of charge at the shop. She left the key with Mildred at the next house down the road. The older lady waved as Bree pulled out of her long gravel drive with Gabe in the front seat beside her. *What have I done, Lord?* Bree didn't look back as she headed south...toward sanctuary.

One

BREE TREHEARN HAD NEVER REALIZED HOW DARK A NIGHT could be until now. Back in Indiana on the farm roads, the darkness had always had a velvety quality to it. Dark had been safe and friendly, a welcoming part of God's handiwork. This tropical dark she was in now felt almost menacing.

Sanibel Island was mostly resorts, wasn't it? So why weren't there any streetlights? She pushed back her long, pale hair. There had been plenty of light on that golf course she'd passed a little earlier. And the strip of restaurants along the main streets had been positively glowing with neon. But now, when she needed the light to try to figure out what was wrong with the car, it was as dark as the inside of a cow and just as welcoming.

She knew she should probably stay inside the car and wait for someone to come along and help her. Only problem with that idea was there hadn't been anybody else on this road in quite a while. Probably because it was so dark. No, she was going to have to get out. Maybe she could find the flashlight under all the other stuff in the backseat and start trying to decipher what it was the car had been trying to tell her when all those little warning lights went on before everything quit.

Bree got out of the car, noticing that the inside light still worked. It was a comforting little glow in all the darkness. With the door open, the foreign nature of everything around her came back again in the gusts of salty breeze on her face and the warmth of the air around her. She had to be crazy to be doing this. But then she'd felt a little crazy since at least Kentucky, so there was nothing new in the feeling.

She walked around and opened the passenger door, pulling the front seat back to try to shift a box or two. That flashlight had to be here somewhere. "Now stay right there," she cautioned Gabe. It was the wrong thing to do. His wide blue eyes opened even wider and he was out of the car like a shot. For a moment he was a pale blur in the dark; then he was gone.

"Oh, Gabe, no. Come back here. You'll get lost.

Gabriel!" Her high, panicky words seemed to hang in the warm, humid air.

"Did you hear something?" Shawn asked, his headlight making a pool for Cody North to trace the bumpy path in front of their racing bikes.

"Yeah. Maybe gulls. Maybe a person. Couldn't tell." Cody started to tell the kid to be quiet, then stopped. Shawn was at that age where he took everything as a personal reproof, even the things Cody never meant that way. So he'd become careful at phrasing things as neutrally as possible. It seemed the best way to get what he wanted without continual ruffled feathers.

They rounded the bend in the path and Shawn pointed to what Cody had already seen. The car was half in the bike path, half at the edge of the street, doors flung open and inside lights on.

Although it seemed to be packed to the roof with stuff, there was no person inside. "This doesn't look so good, sport." Cody coasted to a stop.

"I know. Want me to go look for a phone?"

"Not yet. Let's look around first. Together, okay?" Cody raised his voice to Shawn, who was already abandoning the bike to head into trouble. The kid's daredevil nature would probably serve him well if he went into the service like he said he was going to—that or he'd get blown to bits. Cody winced at the thought. He hadn't gotten to be a thirty-two-year-old ex-cop by leaping into the face of danger. Even as a rookie he suspected he'd had more caution than Shawn did now. Or maybe it was just fear. Whatever it was, it had saved his skin a few times.

He got off his own bike and walked around the car. No one was there, not even on the floorboards. A little way down the path, the sound they'd heard before came again. This time it was definitely human.

"Hellooooo!" Cody hoped whoever was out there was friendly, or at least unarmed if they were as crazy as they sounded. In a moment, a pale shape came racing out of the darkness. "Lost?"

The young woman who was faintly illuminated by the car's dome light looked lost. Her pale hair swirled around her like a demented cloud and her wide eyes looked panicky. "I sure am. But I'm more worried about Gabe. When I opened the door he jumped out of the car and took off. I can't find him."

"Is this an adult we're talking about?"

The woman shook her head. "No. He's a three-year-old white male—"

"We'll help you look." Cody cut her off before she got into more description. No sense in panicking her more by pointing out that this trail and road turned a hundred yards farther, opening onto public beach. If they didn't find this kid soon, he could be walking in the ocean. Or worse. "Can Gabe swim?"

He hadn't thought it possible, but she went another shade paler. "No. He doesn't even like water. But he isn't—"

Cody turned to Shawn. "You go down the street, calling. I'll go down the path toward the public access. We'll meet up there either way, okay?"

Shawn nodded. "Fine."

Cody got back on his bike and started pedaling slowly. He strained his eyes in the darkness for some scrap of clothing, adjusting his eyes down to three-year-old height. Why did it have to be a kid? He hated looking for kids.

He muttered softly under his breath. He hadn't thought to ask what the kid was wearing. No time to go back now. "Gabe." His voice rang out in the darkness. Coasting to a halt and putting down one foot, he looked around. Far in the distance there were lights from beach houses and a resort hotel. But closer in there were just saw grass and sea oats and darkness.

Starting up again, he went a little farther down the path, still calling. There was a rustle in the grass toward his right and he stopped the bike. "Gabe?" Instead of an answer there was more rustling. He headed toward the waist-high grass. As he parted it, something screamed like a panther and a blur of white hurtled toward him, landing on his shoulder.

The momentum of the blow knocked Cody back on his seat, hard. Swearing, trying to hold on to twenty pounds of unhappy cat—with all claws apparently intact—he got up. The spotty clouds overhead chose that moment to give way to rain. Cody held up the furry face in front of him for inspection. "If you're Gabe, she's got some explaining to do."

By the time they got back to the trailhead, Cody and his squirming furry companion were both soaked. "Gabe!" The woman all but crooned the creature's name as she plucked him from Cody's battle-scarred arms. "Oh, baby, you're so wet."

She looked at Cody as if for an explanation. Cody bit his lip. Hard. It was the only way he kept from letting her have it. "In case you hadn't noticed—" he ground each word out carefully—"it's raining." He narrowed his eyes. "And one more thing. Gabe is a *cat*."

"I never said he was human." The young woman could pout with the best of them. She cooed over the wet cat and put him back in her car.

So she was more worried about a wet cat than a wet, scratched cat rescuer. Common sense didn't seem to be big on her list of priorities. Cody shook his head and stalked to the nearest overhang. Since it didn't provide much protection, they were all still getting wet. At least he had the sense to try to come in out of the rain.

Looking around, he tossed his keys to Shawn. "Go home and get dry. I'll be there as soon as I can." The kid was so wet he didn't argue for a change, just pocketed the keys, got on his bike, and left. Cody turned his focus back to the woman.

"You may not have said he was human, but why on earth didn't you tell me he was a cat? I could have broken my neck out there looking for that fuzzball." Said fuzzball had deposited himself in the car's back window well and was giving himself a thorough grooming.

"You didn't give me time. You just charged out of here before I could say anything more about Gabe. It was not my intention that you track down my cat." She stopped, shaking her head.

Running a hand through that impossibly pale hair, she leaned against a cinder-block building that held the public beach offices. "Listen to me. I should thank you for saving my best friend. Instead, I'm getting caught in the same bad-manners trap you seem to find yourself in—"

That was enough. Cody couldn't take it anymore. "Look, lady, I'm wet, I'm tired, and I've been chasing a cat. Manners aren't high on my list right now."

"I know, and I'm sorry for my part in causing you trouble, Mr.—"

"North. Cody North."

"And I'm Bree. I should be offering to pay you or

17

something. Not that I could pay you much because I
don't have much with me. I've been driving since
Yorktown, Indiana, and I think I've spent just about
everything I had on gas."

"Yeah, well, you didn't spend enough of it that
way." A quick examination of the car when she'd tossed
the cat in had told him that among other things, the car
was out of fuel.

"And I feel really stupid about that. I guess I just got
occupied with other things for a while, like where I was
going and finding a place to sleep and everything." She
looked up at the sky; rain was still coming down steadily.
"Guess this dumps on my plan to sleep on the beach."

If Cody thought he'd been upset before, this
pushed him over the edge. "Sleep on the beach? Lady,
are you *nuts*? There are great big signs all over telling
you it's illegal."

Bree stiffened. "Which I can't even see, much less
read, thanks to the lack of lights around here."

"Even without the laws, you'd have to be crazy to
sleep on a public beach. Not only are there all kinds of
animal predators out during the night, it's just not safe
for a young woman." *A beautiful young woman… North!
Keep your mind on business!*

"I have my attack cat." She still looked as defiant as
anyone who resembled a water sprite could look. "And
God's protection."

18

Oh, great! She not only looked like a water sprite, she sounded like a trusting four-year-old. "Some attack cat." It was lame, but it kept him from berating her. It also kept him silent on his opinion of her Pollyanna concept of God. He wasn't ready to go there yet.

Cody looked again to where Gabe was curled up in the window well. From this distance he reminded Cody of the business end of a dust mop. "Don't you have somebody to stay with? reservations somewhere?"

She shook her head. "I was just seeing how far I could get. It was supposed to be a little more organized than it ended up, but it seemed like a good idea at the time. The one night I stopped, there was this great rest area in Georgia. The wind in the pines was wonderful."

"You slept in a highway rest area?"

She bristled again. "I locked the car. And remember, it wasn't like I was alone or anything."

"Right. You had your attack cat and your guardian angel or whatever."

"I take it you have a problem with that?"

If he was smart, he'd ignore the sweetly sarcastic inquiry. But this woman was grating on his nerves like a piece of foil on a filling. She was what his mother would call an innocent. It was about time someone introduced her to reality.

For a moment he considered giving in to the growing need to shake her until her perfect teeth rattled. He was losing the battle with each word out of her mouth. It would be so much easier just to walk away, leaving her to whatever crazy fate she'd called down on herself. Who knew, maybe this Bree—he frowned...what kind of sprouts-and-granola name was *that*, anyway?—was one of those people God actually took care of. There had to be some on the planet. Besides, that image of his mother that Bree's words called up just wouldn't let him walk away. Laura North would have taken her in. It was the *Christian* thing to do. And Laura was a Christian who did the right thing and would give him a hard time if she found out he did otherwise.

He sighed and straightened his shoulders. "Wait here. I need to make a phone call." Shawn should just about be home by now, and he always jumped at a chance to drive the truck. Tonight was going to be his big moment.

An hour later Cody was still asking himself how he had gone from taking a quiet bike ride in the dark to sitting in the back of his own truck getting rained on while surrounded by a strange woman's belongings. When they pulled to a stop at the complex, he jumped out and started handing things to Shawn. "Put her behind the office." Cody watched Shawn's wide-eyed nod. So he thought it was a crazy idea, too.

Couldn't be helped. This girl was a menace, true, but she was probably honest enough. No harm in giv-

ing her the room behind the office until morning. Then
he'd lend her enough for a tank of gas and she could be
on her way.

She seemed to be winding down after her night's
adventures. She looked like a sleepy little kid standing
there outside the truck on the white parking lot, holding the bedraggled cat.

"Come on, I'll show you to your room." She followed quietly enough as they went through the small
office and into the back. "I know it's not much, but it's
warm and dry. There are towels in the bathroom closet
and clean sheets for the sofa bed."

"You're just letting me stay here? For nothing?"

"Overnight." Cody folded his arms and leaned
against the office door. "Tomorrow we'll go rescue
your car before the cops tow it away."

She looked up, a frown wrinkling her brow.
"Aren't you a police officer? I thought from the way
you acted—"

Cody shook his head. "Not anymore. And not here.
No, I just run the condo complex here. I rent vacation
units, not chase bad guys. I do have friends on the
force, and before I go to bed I'll call them and let them
know about your car. That way it will still be there
when it gets light and we go get it started."

"That would be wonderful." The cat walked around
the room, purposefully sniffing each new piece of

furniture he encountered. Without the large furry creature in her arms, Bree looked even tinier. "Cody? Thanks a lot. This is the kindest thing anybody's done for me in a long time."

Cody felt anything but kind. "I'm just keeping you from sleeping on the beach." Bree's answer was to put slender arms around his neck and hug him. It was a warm, sisterly hug. But the contact, brief as it was, left him stunned. He never was certain afterward what he'd said to warrant it, but then did any man really understand women? He fled the room to take refuge in his own house across the yard.

It was only after the bacon was sizzling in the morning that Bree had second thoughts about going into a strange man's house to cook breakfast for him. With him being an ex-cop and all, he might not take kindly to people wandering around his kitchen looking for the coffee filters.

Still, there hadn't been any food in the suite where she'd spent the night, and she hadn't eaten since sometime the day before, early in the day. When the sun rose, Bree hadn't been able to ignore her stomach talking to her anymore.

If he wanted people to stay out of his house, he should keep it locked, she reasoned, flipping one of the strips of bacon in the heavy iron skillet. She'd left Gabe next door. He had his kitty kibble already so he wasn't going to complain. At least she'd remembered to bring that and his litter box out of the car the night before.

Bree wondered again what had possessed her crazy cat to go shooting out of the car in the dark. Usually Gabe was the calmest animal she knew. And he wasn't much of an outside cat. Maybe it had been the different-entness of it all. She was still marveling at the exotic surroundings herself. She would have to ask Cody when he got up what those huge purple flowers were outside the window.

"I should have figured prowlers don't cook break-fast," rumbled a gravelly voice behind her. Bree whirled, bacon fork still in hand.

Her heart pounded in her chest. She was definitely not up for anybody sneaking up behind her. "Did you have to scare me like that?"

The noise that came out of Cody was a growl. "Me? Scare you? How do you think I felt waking up to strange noises in my kitchen?"

"The door wasn't locked. If you want to keep people out, you should lock your door."

He opened his mouth and glared at the door. "It *was* locked."

No need to make him crawl. Bree smiled sweetly. "It was open. I don't break into anybody's house."

Cody sighed. "It should have been locked." His tone was not the least bit gracious, but Bree felt glee. Cody watched her carefully. Did he expect her to gloat?

She smiled again instead, knowing it would drive him nuts. For the first time Bree really noticed that Cody must have charged straight out of bed to defend his castle. Nobody would do anything but sleep in shorts and a T-shirt that looked that ratty. And he wasn't a morning person. That much was clear from his rumpled hair and the dazed look in his dark eyes.

She felt an odd softening inside, almost tenderness. "I didn't mean to get you up like this. Really. I wanted to thank you for your hospitality, not scare you." Why was she apologizing to this man? The last thing she needed was to get caught up with somebody like Cody. He was an ex-cop with all those conscientious Boy Scout tendencies to check up on people. That was enough reason to keep her emotional distance right there.

Cody ran a hand through his hair. It didn't straighten any. "Aw, forget it. Shawn came in last. I expected him to lock up. Obviously he didn't."

She realized he was watching her and started talking nervously. "I'm really sorry. It's just that there wasn't any coffee in the apartment, and besides, I thought it would be nice to pay you back for all your help last night by making breakfast."

He softened a little at her apology, looking slightly less like a riled porcupine. "I guess so. But if you do it again, warn me. Sneaking up on somebody who spent a decade wearing a gun isn't a great idea."

"I'll remember the next time." She wondered if there would ever be a next time. Cody had been ready to get rid of her last night, which was a shame. This was a wonderful place, and she'd love a few days to explore it.

"Your bacon's burning." His laconic comment sent her back to the stove in a hurry and drove thoughts of exploring the beach out of her mind.

After a few minutes Shawn came into the kitchen. Bree smiled at him. "Still got a few more days of school?" Nobody dressed this sharply on summer vacation.

The boy nodded. In full daylight she could tell all kinds of things about him that she hadn't been able to see the night before. Whatever his relationship to Cody, it didn't appear to be by blood. His coppery skin and high cheekbones hinted at Native American ancestry, and the startlingly green eyes that looked back at her were vastly different from Cody's golden brown ones.

It gave a new dimension to both of them to see Cody and Shawn sitting at the breakfast table.

Cody snatched a piece of bacon off the plate before Shawn wolfed them all down. "Finals?"

"Three."

"Studied?"

"Yep."

"Need any more help?"

"Not this time. I'll be back by two-thirty." Bree wondered if they always spoke in this male shorthand, or it if was because of her presence in the kitchen. Whatever the case, Shawn seemed grateful for a hot breakfast before he took off. He even took his own dishes to the sink without being reminded, then made quick good-byes and loped out the door.

"School bus picks him up at the corner. They go across to the mainland for high school." Cody sipped his coffee, answering Bree's question before she asked it. "If we want to get your car going, we'll have to do it pretty early. I've got a business to run and the office needs to be open by nine."

"Will do." Bree rose from her seat at the table. The kitchen was all she'd seen of Cody's house, but it suited him. Everything was spare and trim, with the walls and fixtures a pale sand color and accents of beach colors like brown and coral. It was clearly a man's decorating scheme, and Bree had to admit that secretly it relieved her. For a moment when she let herself in to make breakfast she wondered if she was going to run into another woman. But this kitchen was obviously the domain of a single male.

She went to her room and was ready in record time. Gabe grumbled around her ankles, anxious to go with her, but she shooed him aside as she shut the door. "No sense in letting you get out again," she said. He went off somewhere to sulk, and Bree hoped he didn't decide to vent any of his frustration on the sofa bed that she'd slept on the night before. That would guarantee that Cody wouldn't let her stay.

He was in the office going over a stack of papers when she came out. "Problems?" *As if he'd tell her if there were.* Cody North didn't look like the type who shared his worries even with friends, much less strangers.

"Not really. I'm just trying to figure out where one bike we rented out last week is. The paperwork seems to have disappeared. That was what Shawn and I were doing last night, a recovery trip." His grin didn't hold any humor. "We go around looking for our overdue rentals. When and if we find them, we put our locks on them or move them to another location. Then in the morning we come and pick them up."

"So what's the problem with your missing one?" Bree looked around the office and frowned. Where was the man's computer? "All you have to do is call up its ID number on your hard drive and it should pop right up, shouldn't it?"

His forehead creased. Bree marveled that even a scowl was attractive on this man. This spelled danger for sure, but she didn't have time to worry about that now. "It would pop up. If it was on the hard drive. If, indeed, Island Breeze Condos had a hard drive. I assume that's part of a computer?"

She sat down on the office chair in the corner. "You're kidding. How can you run a business of this size without one?"

His jaw tensed as though he was grinding his teeth. How could she be so adept at frustrating him? "We've managed so far."

"Well, you'd manage a lot better with a computer." An idea percolated in Bree's fertile brain. She knew that was another bad sign, but this idea sounded like a good one. "In fact, I could prove it to you. One of the things in my car is a spare PC. It's a really nice setup, and I could put your records on it and show you. Give me a couple days and I'll prove to you that you should have done this a long time ago."

"What I should have done is not mention it." Cody laughed. "So why am I going to say yes?"

"Because you seem to be a competent business owner and an all-around good guy. And a super father." Bree bounded up out of the chair, trying to suppress the urge to hug him in her delight at convincing him so easily.

"Father? What has Shawn got to do with this?"

"How can any high schooler get by without a computer these days? Next semester those papers are going to be a snap if you keep the computer."

Cody shook his head. "Those papers will never be a snap." He paused, settling back into his chair. "But you're right about one thing; Shawn would like the computer. Come on, let's go get the gasoline and get that car moving. You can follow me back here."

"And set up the computer?" The darkening of his glare told her she should leave it alone, but she just couldn't. She wasn't sure why, but she really wanted to do this.

When she didn't backpedal, he sighed. "Fine. Set up your blasted computer. But don't expect miracles."

"You won't regret this," Bree promised as they went out the door.

"Now there's where you're wrong. I already regret it." Cody unlocked the truck for her. "I have a feeling you engender that reaction in a lot of people."

In that moment she almost told him about Bo. If anybody regretted dealing with her, it would be him. Cody looked like he could handle somebody as scary as Bo, but she wasn't ready yet to involve anybody else in her mess. "I almost forgot. Those big purple things right outside my window. What are they?"

Cody started the truck before he started his lecture on Florida plant life. As they backed out of the lot at Island Breeze, Bree gave a silent sigh of relief. She was safe for another day.

Two

IT TOOK ONLY HALF A DAY FOR BREE TO INSERT HERSELF into every area of running the Island Breeze vacation complex. *How does she do that?* Cody saw it happen but couldn't figure it out. If he tried it, he would feel like a fake.

When he bought into the Island Breeze complex and became the manager, it had taken him weeks to get along with the office staff—and months for him to get to know the other employees like grounds crew and maintenance. But this was Bree's first day in the office, and by the time Cody had gone to the house, fixed lunch, and brought the woman a tuna sandwich and some chips, she was laughing with the cleaning crew as if they were old friends.

"They're adorable, Marisa." Bree smiled at the shy,

quiet woman from Mexico. Cody hadn't gotten a full sentence out of Marisa since hiring her a month before. "All three of them. Cody, aren't these the cutest kids you've ever seen?"

Marisa seemed to shrink even more than her slight five feet when Cody looked over her shoulder at the pictures. "Sure are." He put Bree's sandwich plate on the desk. "Better let the ladies get to work, though, so they can stop and have lunch soon, too."

"I know, but I couldn't resist getting to know everybody. And you brought me lunch. This is dolphin-safe tuna, I hope."

"Sure." Did that actually matter to anybody? He and Shawn looked for cheap tuna. Dolphin would just be extra protein.

"This looks great." Bree looked down at her plate. "So in addition to your other talents you cook too, huh?"

Cody stifled a laugh. "If you call tuna salad cooking, I do. Actually I do okay in that arena. My mom made it very clear to her sons that cooking and cleaning were survival skills."

"Good for her. Remind me to send her a thank-you note sometime. It's nice to have a boss who can cook."

"Boss?" This woman was unbelievable. "Exactly when did I hire you?" The last he knew he was just feeding her and giving her a place to stay for a day or two;

then she was moving on. Obviously she had different ideas.

"Well, you do look shorthanded." Bree looked around the empty office.

"That's just because Charlotte has the day off. I am definitely not hiring somebody I found on the beach last night."

"So you'll let me sleep here for free, but you won't hire me?" Bree folded her arms and arched an eyebrow. "What about I work for free in exchange for room and board?"

Cody shook his head. "State employment people would have my hide. No, if I put Shawn on the payroll to keep them happy, I'd have to put you on, too."

"Does Shawn work here after school?"

"Summer vacations. He starts the day after finals are over, working with the grounds crew."

"Working outside, getting to use riding mowers. Tough life when you're seventeen, huh?"

Cody couldn't believe Bree's connection with people. She had an empathy that seemed almost instant with folks. "Yeah, I guess. He does a good job, though. And he's putting away money for college."

"Does he know what he wants to do?"

"He knows what he thinks he wants." Not that it was this woman's business. Cody knew he was scowling. "According to Shawn, the moment he graduates he's going into the service and let them train him in either law enforcement or electronics."

"Doesn't look like dad agrees with that one."

"I can think of places I'd rather have him. But once he's eighteen he doesn't need me to sign for him. Just like I didn't need my mom to sign for me for the police academy at twenty-one, even though she wasn't thrilled when I went."

"It is dangerous. I'm sure I don't have to point that out."

Cody spoke up before she started sounding any more like his mother. "Not to me you don't. But anything can be dangerous. My father was a desk jockey his entire life and died of a heart attack."

"I'm sorry." Bree sat up straighter and opened those huge blue eyes even wider, if that was possible. "But still, you have to admit moms worry about their sons, especially when going to work means strapping on a magnum, or whatever it was you carried, and going out to defend people."

"That sounds a lot more glamorous than what I remember of most police work." Cody shook his head. He remembered a lot of paperwork and bad coffee, and very little defending people. "You want another sandwich?"

Bree looked down. She seemed to be surprised that the plate in front of her was empty. "No, I guess not. This one was delicious. I guess I was hungrier than I thought. But I do need to get back to work here."

"And what, may I ask, are you doing?" Cody looked around at the parts of a computer strung around the office.

"Figuring out how best to set things up here to make it efficient for you, or for whoever is working the desk. Once I get the hardware all hooked up, it will be time to start inputting files."

Well, that had probably been in English, Cody decided, but it made less sense to him than the Spanish Marisa and Lucy traded back and forth between units as they worked. "Fine. You just keep working on setting this up." At least she wasn't off thinking about sleeping on the beach, or losing that dust mop she called a cat. Anything else was probably going to be more peaceful.

Bree looked around the office at Island Breeze. *If only I could stay here...*

It was so peaceful. The place was organized and pleasant, despite not having a computer. It was more organized, she had to admit, than her own jumbled work space attached to the tiny house she'd rented in Indiana. Of course, her work space was always filled with other people's files and computer parts, and her own projects as well. No wonder Cody could keep things neat. He only had to deal with renting condos to vacationers, and he had a part-time office person to help do that.

Bree looked forward to meeting Cody's assistant. He'd told her that Charlotte came in every day, except Monday, from eleven to four to keep things going. "And she's going to love this whole setup." Cody waved an arm over the computer Bree continued to assemble. "She's been after me for quite a while to get one. Said her husband's church office could hardly function without theirs."

"So she's a pastor's wife. Do you attend their church?"

Cody looked away from her. "Once in a while. When I get time. Shawn goes to youth group things there." From his expression, Bree judged that Shawn was seen inside the church building a lot more than his father.

"Where is it? I'd love to check it out." She decided not to make Cody squirm any more. At least not yet.

"Island Community Church, just off Periwinkle about halfway through town."

"Isn't everything on or just off Periwinkle?" Bree chuckled. "I'm sure there are other streets on the island, but the other night when I was driving through it seemed like no matter where I went, I eventually ended up back on Periwinkle."

"It is the main drag. And Ed, Charlotte's husband, is glad to have such a solid location for the church. He gets a lot of tourists walking in every week as well as the locals. You'll probably like it there. It's a friendly place."

Bree took a breath, ready to tell Cody that a friendly atmosphere was nice, but it wasn't the most important thing she looked for in a church. *Maybe I'd better hold that lecture till another time.* Cody already appeared put off by any mention of God or religion. No sense in making him more hostile.

Besides, she had other things to think about. She'd chosen this area to keep a low profile, not to go to the most popular church around. That might get her noticed almost as fast as signing on to the Internet and updating her now-abandoned home page for BiTs & Pieces.

Still, she felt God's hand had led her to this place. Cody clearly needed her help…and his assistant was a pastor's wife with a friendly church. If she had to lay low for a while, this place seemed to be almost custom-designed as a refuge.

"Were you about to say something?" Cody raised one dark eyebrow. So he was observant along with his quiet demeanor. Bree shook her head, troubled. She had to watch herself around Cody. The last thing she needed was him getting curious and starting to dig into who she was. And where she'd come from.

"No, nothing." She shuffled the stack of papers in front of her. "Do you want to stick around and get your first lesson on how this computer works? I'm about to turn it on and see how everything goes."

"No, thanks. I'm pretty sure I heard the school bus. Time to catch Shawn as he gets home and see how day one of finals went."

"Fine. I'll talk to you later." Bree watched him lope out the door onto the parking lot. From what she'd seen, he was a good father to Shawn. She wondered how long he'd been at it. A while, judging from the easy relationship between the two of them. Some natural parents of high school boys didn't seem as comfortable in their role as Cody did.

Bree reached down under the desk and plugged in the surge-protector strip that all the hardware was plugged into. Switching on the power, it was good to hear the reassuring hum of the computer as it booted up.

Watching everything flicker on in the usual way, Bree realized that this was just the beginning. Once she'd gotten all of Cody's business files loaded onto the hard drive, she could start designing a home page for Island Breeze. Clearly a man who didn't bother with a computer for the essentials like bookkeeping wasn't advertising on the Internet, either. She had her work cut out for her.

It didn't take long to get the computer up and running. Bree smiled in satisfaction; then her gaze drifted to the tower. She cast a quick glance around to be sure she was alone, then unscrewed and removed the metal case of the tower. A breath of relief escaped her. The diskettes were there, snug in their plastic bag taped to the side of the metal housing. She pulled them free, then slid one into the drive. She was still alone, with time to check the second disk as well. A glance at their contents told her they were still intact. She quickly scanned both diskettes, then put them back where they had been.

Her instincts still told her to throw the disks away. To get as far from the evil they held as humanly possible. But she knew that wouldn't be the right thing to do. The right thing would be what she'd done already.

Well, almost. To truly do the right thing, she should find an FBI agent, or somebody from the ATF or something, and turn these hideous things over.

She bit her lip. If turning the files over didn't lead to Bo's immediate arrest, he would be after her like a shot. At best, turning those disks over to the authorities would tell him for sure what Bree knew he already suspected—that when she repaired his computer, she also cracked his code and deciphered his files.

"I know your protection is all around me, Lord," she murmured as she put the case back on the computer.

"Help me trust it as far as I need to, because right now nothing feels safe."

She looked around the office again. It was so warm, so calm and peaceful. If only she could just stay here and ignore her problem. It would be so much easier than what she knew she had to do. Eventually.

But for now she was going to enjoy the warmth and peace. She was going to get this computer functional and start some business files for Cody. The rest would have to wait for a while.

She was out there somewhere. Bo knew it as certainly as he knew that she wasn't coming back to the shop in Yorktown. How could Bree, of all people, have betrayed him like this? He pounded one heavy fist against the wall. He didn't do it hard enough to put a hole in the flimsy wallboard, but hard enough to vent some of his growing anger. Bree might have left town, but she was still around someplace. And she had taken what he needed with her. Of that he was certain. He had to find her, quickly. The only problem was, he had no idea where to look.

When Charlotte came in the next day, she seemed ecstatic. Bree wasn't sure what Cody's assistant was happier about——the computer or having company in the office.

"This is great." Charlotte ran her hands over the computer. "I've been telling that stubborn boss of mine for ages that we need a computer. I've also been telling him we need more help around here. Talk about answers to prayers."

Bree liked her bubbly new coworker on sight. She was probably in her late forties, with reddish hair and a slightly rounded figure she said came from "too many church potlucks." Unlike Cody, Charlotte had a ready smile and warm brown eyes that sparkled when he introduced her to Bree, and kept on sparkling the rest of the morning.

Bree learned more about the business operation in half an hour from Charlotte than she had in a whole day with Cody. Of course, Charlotte said more, period, in half an hour than Cody had in the previous two days

Cody moved through the office, sparing only a glance for the two of them. "Time to start on the outside stuff." He was out the door quickly.

Bree turned to Charlotte. "Is Cody always so quiet?"

"Usually. If there's a subject Cody North is voluble on, I don't know about it. Ed always says God gave us two ears and one mouth for a good reason, but frankly I think Cody overuses his ears and neglects his mouth."

Bree stifled a giggle. She'd already come to the same conclusion, but it was good to hear it voiced by someone who knew him better. "And he's so serious."

Bree imitated the frown that so often appeared on Cody's face, and Charlotte giggled.

"That will change a little once you get settled in around here." Charlotte patted her hand. "He has a wicked sense of humor. Only trouble is, you won't be able to tell when he's joking, at least not by his expressions. He's always as straight-faced as ever."

"Oh, great. One of those," Bree muttered.

"He'll grow on you." Charlotte gave her another pat with a soft, plump hand.

Oh no, he won't. I'll do what you want, Lord, but I won't care about Cody. I don't need anybody else to care about now. Especially anybody as enigmatic and irritating as her new boss. Sure, he was also very attractive in his own way, but she could ignore that, couldn't she? Right now it was all she could do to keep Gabe happy and in kitty litter and herself working and out of trouble. No sense adding to her problems by letting Cody grow on her.

"So tell me about Ed and the church." Better to distract Charlotte with another subject. That way she wouldn't have to admit any attraction to their disturbing boss.

"Oh, he is the sweetest man." From the way Charlotte lit up, you'd think they were newlyweds. "We've been married twenty-seven years, since he was a starving seminarian and I was a skinny young coed who starved along with him. Not that you could tell it now." She laughed, looking down ruefully at the ample figure sheathed in pink cotton. Bree had to laugh with her at that remark. And she really wanted to know about Charlotte's church, so she had no problem listening and nodding while Charlotte told her all about Ed and his flock.

Cody pulled his vehicle into the parking lot at Island Breeze with a deep sigh. What a day. Nowhere near noon, and plenty of problems already. He reached up to rub at the knots in his shoulder muscles, wincing as he did so, then headed for the office.

He pushed open the door and came to an abrupt halt. Bree and Charlotte were laughing and chatting like co-conspirators. Great. Just what he needed, these two smart alecks arrayed against him. That they would somehow join forces, even in a friendly way, he had no doubt. Women seemed to view him as a challenge.

Right now he had to break up the party to find out something important. "Bree? Ms. Trehearn? Hello?" His voice escalated in volume with each word until he finally got her attention.

Bree just stared at him. She must have learned that look from her demented cat. Her blue eyes were feline wide and seemed surprised that she was being summoned. "Yes, Cody. What can I do for you?"

Get in your car and head for the mainland, Cody was tempted to say. Just talking to her made him break out in a prickly sweat. Bree Trehearn was unlike anybody he'd had to deal with in a long time, and she...bothered him. No, that wasn't quite right. She irritated him...got under his skin...worked on his nerves like a song you can't get out of your mind. And every time she aimed that gaze in his direction, he wasn't sure which need was stronger: to gather her up and hold her close—or to turn and bolt out the door.

Okay. So she scared him spitless. But he wasn't going to admit that to her. Not now, probably not ever.

Intimidating. That was the word to describe Cody. It popped into Bree's head with his first question when he came back into the office.

"Do you speak Spanish?"

Wonderful. Another area of deficiency to admit to this man. She laughed. "No, not past the restaurant variety and what I remember from high school, which feels like eons ago. I don't speak Spanish, but the computer does, a little. Why?"

Cody's frown was the grumpiest yet. "Well, in case you haven't noticed, Lucy's English isn't that great, and Marisa's is even worse. Not that anything stopped you from communicating with them yesterday."

ISLAND BREEZE

It was on the tip of her tongue to tell him not to be snide about it, but that wouldn't help matters any; and for a change Cody looked like he had a serious problem to solve. "Lucy's a little shy, and Marisa is very quiet."

"Whatever." Cody waved off her comments. "How can that machine speak Spanish if nobody here does?"

Now this I know. "Easy. You can load foreign language programs that will translate. I've been thinking about teaching myself Spanish for a while so that I could start helping out in a church program back home."

"You have bilingual programs up there?" Charlotte interrupted, as she did often. "Ed wants to get something going here too, but we haven't gotten to it yet. He speaks the language better than I do, by the way." She glanced at Cody.

"What do you need?" Bree asked.

Cody grimaced. It was probably that word *need.* Cody didn't look like the type to need anything. "I need you to make a sign. We need to make sure Marisa and Lucy are aware of a spot of termite damage that I just found on one of the stairwells outside. If anybody pushed up against the railing on the landing between levels of Jacaranda, they could go straight through. Just something simple that says 'Danger' or whatever. I know the tenants will pay attention if I post it in English, but I don't know about Lucy and Marisa."

Charlotte nodded and turned to Bree, who looked

puzzled. "You haven't been around the complex much yet, have you? The units are four to a building, and each building has a name, as well as a number. Jacaranda is number 5, the far one over to the east end of the complex."

"If you say so." Bree shrugged. "I need to wander around some today, get to know where I'm going. But first I can get into the beginning Spanish program and see what I find."

"And I can call Ed." Charlotte walked to her desk and started dialing.

Cody shook his head. "It will never be boring, will it?"

"What?"

"Life around you. Tell Charlotte I'm going to the hardware store, and keep Marisa and Lucy on the ground."

"Will do, boss." Bree couldn't resist adding that last bit, even though it earned her a frown.

"Hi, sweetheart." Bree heard Charlotte on the phone as Cody left the building. "How do you say *danger* or *dangerous* in Spanish? Me neither, but Cody needs to know..."

Cody shook his head. No, things were not going to get boring around here anytime soon. Maybe that was all right. He'd felt life slipping into a rut in the last few months. What was it Dave had always said? The only difference between a rut and a grave was depth.

Dave.

A pang of loss struck Cody so hard he felt his heart jump. He clenched his teeth. It had been five years. You'd think by now he would have gotten past the pain that came with thoughts of his partner. But he hadn't gotten past it.

Not by a long shot.

Three

BREE LOOKED AROUND THE COMPLEX IN CONSTERNATION.
How was she supposed to tell Lucy and Marisa about
the damaged railing if she couldn't even find them?
Shouldn't they be at work by now? Lucy's car wasn't in
the lot anywhere that she could see. What did she do
now? She told Cody she'd keep them on the ground
and away from that landing.

She could still make the sign and post it. That
would warn them if she didn't find them. Bree looked
around the complex one more time. Surely she just
wasn't looking in the right places. *So go in and make the
sign.* Ten minutes later Bree decided that wonderful as
computers were, they weren't the tool for in-depth
foreign language study. *Danger* was easy to find, but *termites?* Impossible. Sighing, she gave up. The sign she

printed out just said Danger. *Pelligro.* No entrance. *No Entrada.* No work of art, but it would have to do.

Where did Charlotte keep the duct tape? Bree couldn't find anything but regular clear tape she would have to use to tape this inadequate sign to a regular wall. She had to do this for Cody. Regular tape would have to suffice. Grabbing a couple of pieces, she stuck them to the sign.

It was sticky-hot outside already. Bree missed the morning cool back home in Indiana. Just walking across the complex to Jacaranda made sweat drip down her back. And once she got there, she couldn't find a decent place to put up her sign. She stuck it to the stair railing that climbed to the landing. Not a great place for it, but it was the only place where the wood was wide enough for that puny tape to stick.

She headed back to her cool office. Halfway there she thought about making another all-out effort to find the cleaning crew. Just stopping to stand still and think made the heat oppressive. Surely Lucy and Marisa would stop by the office first. And if they didn't, she had posted the sign. Bree headed for the sanctuary of air-conditioning.

A cool drink and setting up the Island Breeze business accounts took her mind off her worries. That she could do without getting into trouble. At least no more trouble than she was already in.

The bell jingling above the door got her attention. "I'm back," Cody called jauntily as he came into the office. "Did your magic machine solve all the problems around here?" She should be aggravated with the man's attitude. Why couldn't he be more obnoxious, or at least not so good looking? It would be easier to work around him.

"Some of the problems. Not all of them." Cody looked a little closed in when he came into the office. He belonged out in the sunshine, with those shades on the bridge of his nose instead of pushed up on top of his head. He looked like the kind of man who was much more comfortable outside with the breeze ruffling his dark hair.

Actually, she wouldn't mind ruffling his dark hair herself. Bree jerked, stunned. Where had *that* thought come from? The last thing she needed to be doing right now was ruffling anyone's hair, least of all that of a man she'd just met.

Still... Bree glanced at Cody again. She had the suspicion that nobody teased Cody North enough, unless it was his son. The man looked much too serious for his own good. She put that thought away so that she could finish answering his question.

"I can track just about anything in the complex, and by tomorrow we could probably figure out which units will be rented from now until next year this time." Bree saved the document she was working on. "But I didn't have much luck telling Lucy or Marisa about the termites. I couldn't find them."

"But you did make the sign?"

"Sure. I found the word for *danger* in Spanish. No luck on *termites,* though."

"Good. At least you found something. My Spanish is almost nonexistent, and what I do know isn't appropriate for ladies."

"Oh?"

"Yeah, it's definitely police Spanish. When you have to intimidate bad guys, you don't tell them to please be quiet and kindly stand still. It's a little more intense than that."

"I can imagine," she said, breaking out in a grin. The image of Cody spouting gutter Spanish to someone pressed up against a brick wall was easy to come by. He would be imposing in a uniform and dark sunglasses, with that strong, square jaw clenched, arms crossed over his broad chest...

No, stop it! This line of thought would take her straight into trouble. And she had more of that than she could handle already. She really had to keep her mind on something boring, like business.

"Go fix your railing. If you stay in here talking to me, I'm going to bill you for consulting time on the computer."

"Yeah, that'll happen. You look like what my mother would call a soft touch."

"She would probably be right. It's hard for me to say no to anybody. And I'm sure I don't charge enough for most of my repairs." As soon as the words were out, Bree wanted to snatch them back. What was wrong with her? Since when did she tell total strangers about herself—especially about her weaknesses? She narrowed her eyes. What was it about this man that had her ready to spill her life story to him?

"At least you don't give away service for free." Cody's eyes sparkled.

"Not very often." The confession just seemed to come of its own volition. "Only to folks over sixty-five, and the school district once in a while. But their computers are so old it's like a history lesson working on some of them anyway."

Cody grinned. "Definitely a soft touch. Are you planning to charge me for what you're doing here?"

It hadn't entered her mind. "I don't know. If I end up giving you this computer to keep in the office, we'll have to come to some agreement. But right now you're providing me room and board and keeping Gabe at the same time. I can't ask for much, can I?"

Cody shook his head again, and the gentle laughter in his eyes took her breath away. "Way too soft a touch. We're going to have to teach you how to bargain."

Bree closed her eyes. There were a lot of things she could imagine Cody teaching her. Bargaining was the least of them.

Oh, help...

"Really, I mean it. Go out there and get to work."

Cody lost the laughter in his eyes. "Eager to get rid of me, aren't you?"

He had no idea how eager she was.

There was still no sign of Bree. Bo tapped on his desktop, muttering to the screen in front of him. How could he have misjudged her this much? First she hadn't been the compliant little airhead he'd always figured her for. He'd expected her to just make the repairs on his computer and give it back like always. No, she'd done a good deal more than that. Uncovered his secret...stolen his property...and apparently had the smarts to leave the county and hide out.

It didn't add up.

He could understand her leaving the shop and the house. Neither one meant that much to her, especially once Bo found out that she'd finished all her customers' repair jobs and gotten the computers back to her clients before she left in the middle of a dark Indiana night.

She, that stupid cat, the car, and her computer were all gone. That in itself told Bo she wouldn't be back soon. Everything she really valued was with her, wherever she was. So he hadn't found out her location yet; that wasn't a complete surprise. But why wasn't she showing up online? The one other thing he would have said he knew about Bree was her delight in her Web page and all her Internet friends. He'd have laid down money that she wouldn't stay away from those things for long. But she hadn't shown up on the Net at all. Where was Bree Trehearn hiding out that she didn't even go online? Bo swore softly. He shouldn't have called her so many times, or cruised the house. Maybe he'd driven her so far underground he wouldn't be able to find her.

He gritted his teeth. No, that wasn't acceptable. He would find her. And soon.

Friday was Cody's least favorite day around the complex. Most folks were happy and bouncy on Friday because their work week was done and the weekend started. But for him, like anyone who managed vacation property, Friday and Saturday were headache days.

The rental week for the units started and ended on Saturday. That meant any unit that was vacant on Friday got more cleaning than usual in expectation of tenants. Guests were not in the best moods because their vacation was almost over and they had to go back home to Cleveland—or wherever they came from. They were looking for a fax machine and for the closest pack-andship place for all their seashells and souvenirs that didn't fit in their luggage.

On top of it all they were usually sunburned and itchy from the sand-flea bites they had gotten on the beach. The no-see-ums were pretty wicked this time of year too. Cody remembered his first year on the island, when he wasn't used to putting on insect repellant as a matter of course before going outside anytime between April and October. He probably got eaten alive a dozen times before he learned.

Dave had laughed himself sick over that one. For a week after Cody had gone back to Tampa and the job, Dave suggested they could spend their breaks playing connect the dots on Cody's bug bites. Still, Dave had listened when Cody told him about how magical the island was, aside, of course, from the bug population. It was Dave who suggested the two of them start a second career down there when his time was up with the force.

In the end, only Cody made the move. He still didn't understand why Dave had died. Being a cop, Cody had been aware most of the time that death could be just around the corner. However, the death a cop was ready for was one at the end of a chase, when one too many bullets got fired.

Squinting in the hot noonday sun, Cody thought again that he could have handled that, if it had been

Dave's destiny. Given that they were partners, he probably would have gone with him, or at least been there when things went down. As it was he would always have regrets and questions—

Knock it off, North! He shoved a hand through his hair. Why was he going over this again? It always ended the same way, with him feeling angry and empty. What had possessed him to open himself to this train of thought again?

The answer was simple: Bree. She'd possessed him. Or at least his thoughts. Her enthusiasm, her spark for life, her easy way of making friends and sharing herself… Cody saw a part of himself in her, a part he'd lost when Dave died. And watching her, having her around day after day, made him ache inside. She was so young and beautiful. He didn't know whether to pat her on the head and give her milk and cookies—or steal kisses instead.

He hadn't been attracted this way to a woman in years. When he was a police officer he'd played the field a fair amount, never anything serious. Then before he was ready to settle down, Dave died. That was when Cody decided that a God who let things like that happen to a man like Dave didn't deserve Cody's attention. His interest in relationships seemed to wane at the same time.

Bree's trusting face came to mind. How would that

trust vanish? Who would teach her the truth about life, that you can only rely on yourself? With any luck, it wouldn't be him. And when it happened, Cody wanted to be far away from her.

Daydreaming wasn't going to get his work done. There was still the lumber to unload out of the truck. And he needed to get his heavy toolbox up that flight of stairs to the landing of Jacaranda. At least nobody would be up there, thanks to Bree's sign. What he really needed was something like bright yellow crime-scene tape. That would keep anybody from leaning on the railing.

It would have the guests leaving in droves, too. No one appreciated strife or controversy while on vacation. Even routine repairs and maintenance had to be covered up a little to give the visitors the impression that everything about Island Breeze was always in perfect shape. They might tolerate termites at home, but not on vacation.

All around him Cody could hear the noise of a busy day. Cars drove by on Periwinkle, windows down and radios playing. If he listened hard, there were the breakers at the beach. And in the distance, the distinctive sound of Lucy's cart full of cleaning supplies squeaked as she and Marisa got it up a flight of stairs.

Cody frowned. That sound was just a little too far off. The only way that squeak, mixed with the music from Lucy's favorite Spanish radio station, could be that distant was if they were working on Jacaranda—

This couldn't be happening. He should shout across the complex. No, they'd never hear him.

He started out at a run. Before he'd covered half the distance to Jacaranda, the noise he'd been dreading split the sultry air. There was a splintering and a shriek, followed by a thud and a crash. Changing directions, Cody sprinted back to the office in a flash. Sticking his head in the door, he shouted at a startled Charlotte and Bree. "I told you to tell them— Never mind now. Somebody fell! Call 911. Then meet me at unit 5."

Cody's words chilled Bree to the bone. For a moment after his shouted commands, she just sat with her hands poised over the keyboard, not moving, trying to make sense out of what he'd said. An accident? It must be a fairly bad one if he wanted them to call 911.

Bree thanked God that Charlotte was quicker to respond than she was. Charlotte was already on the phone, giving the dispatcher on the other end of the line directions on where in the complex to find unit 5. "I have to go help. And there's no cordless phone, so no, I can't stay on the line," Bree heard Charlotte say in a strained voice. She put down the phone. "Let's go."

Bree made her shaking legs carry her out the door.

"I don't understand, Charlotte. I put up a sign. They shouldn't have gone up there."

Charlotte grabbed Bree's hand. "Who knows what happened. They did go up there, and now we have to keep moving. Pick up some clean towels if we pass Lucy's cart. If there's been an accident bad enough for Cody to want an ambulance, we'll need them."

Bree nodded. She could hear the older woman asking God's protection on the ambulance crew, on everyone in the complex, and on Cody as she strode purposefully across the yard to where Cody leaned over a still figure. Bree could hardly force out a weak amen once in a while following Charlotte, and she didn't really want to look at what was ahead. She already had the sinking feeling she knew what she would see, and it was all her fault.

Cody paused long enough to grab another clean towel from Lucy. This was all his fault. If he had been more forceful about warning Lucy and Marisa himself, none of this would have happened. If he hadn't been distracted by Bree, he would have gotten to the chore faster, but that didn't make this her fault. If he'd been more in control, he wouldn't be straining his ears for the wail of an ambulance siren while Marisa moaned in a language he didn't understand.

"They'll be here soon," he told her, sure that her wild, pain-filled eyes registered nothing he said. It was hard to convince her to keep still. Cody could tell that the ugly compound fracture of her lower leg was going to mean days, if not weeks, in the hospital. He suspected that her left arm was broken as well. How could he have allowed this to happen? How could he have trusted somebody as flaky as Bree to get a message across, when he should have delivered it himself? He should have stayed here and made sure everybody understood this instead of leaving it to Bree and going to the hardware store.

It was all he could do not to point out Bree's precious sign when she ran up to him. Fat lot it did crumpled in the dirt upside down. Lucy and Marisa had probably never seen it. Well, he couldn't fix that now.

Charlotte and Bree were beside him now along with Lucy. While he pressed another towel to Marisa's leg to try to slow the bleeding, the three women knelt by Marisa's head. Charlotte's eyes locked onto his, clearly seeking reassurance.

"911?" He forced a calm into the question that he was far from feeling.

She nodded. "They're on their way. What can we do?"

"Pray," he said without even thinking. They didn't have the medical training to do anything else. He glanced at Bree. Her skin was almost as pale as her platinum hair. "Are we going to need to catch you?" The words came out more harshly than he intended. She jumped, and Cody tried to soften his voice a little. "Because if we are, move now before you faint on top of the patient."

"I'm okay." She swallowed hard. "And I can definitely pray." She looked over at Lucy. "Do you know Jesus?"

Oh, brother! Cody opened his mouth to tell Bree this wasn't the time or the place for preaching, but Lucy's quick nod stopped him.

"*Sí.* I—I mean yes. *Jesus Christo.*" She shook her head and a sob escaped her. "My—my English... *no puede hablar... lo siento...*" She drew a shaky breath and tried again. "I—I am... afraid."

"We all are, Lucy." The gentleness in Bree's voice and in her expression as she talked with Lucy reached out and wrapped itself around Cody's heart. He knew she was talking to calm Lucy, but he found himself listening intently as well. What's more, he almost wanted to believe her. Almost.

"Jesus—*Jesus Christo,* you called him—he's here with us, and we can ask for strength from him to keep Marisa calm and comfortable until the ambulance comes. Can you tell her what we're doing?"

Lucy nodded, then grasped Marisa's right hand.

Leaning down close to her face, she talked softly and swiftly in Spanish. When she stopped, Bree and Charlotte laid their hands on the other two women and started praying. Cody could only watch in amazement as he stanched blood with his towels and the three women prayed over Marisa, who seemed, thankfully, to have passed out.

It was all Cody could do to keep quiet. Did Bree and Charlotte really believe this was helping? True, Lucy was no longer panicked and Bree was no longer pale. Cody studied her as she talked to her Lord, hands outstretched and eyes closed. She looked stronger and more focused than Cody had seen her so far. *What was it like to have that kind of strength, feel that focus on a power greater than what you could touch and see?*

Dave had had that strength, that focus. *And he was just as dead as if he'd had nothing.* Cody's bitterness was so real he could taste it.

Meanwhile his hands and arms ached up into his chest with the effort of keeping just the right amount of pressure on Marisa's leg. He had never heard a sweeter sound than the ambulance when it pulled up into the courtyard behind them.

In a few moments the paramedics had taken over and were stabilizing Marisa, who had regained consciousness. She was trying, in labored Spanish, to tell them something. Lucy nodded and grasped her hand, telling her something in return that seemed to calm her.

"What's going on?" Cody asked.

"Her children. She needs to get them soon from the day care. Their father is gone. And now—"

"Tell her not to worry. Her children will be cared for as long as she is in the hospital," Bree said. "Tell her we'll take them in here, won't we, Cody?"

You could have asked me about that first. He said the only thing that he could. "Of course. And there's a place for her here too once she's out of the hospital and recovering. This shouldn't have happened."

Bree's reaction surprised him. Instead of relief, she looked oddly guilty. "I know." She turned away from him. Was she in tears? "Oh, how I know."

Wordlessly they watched as the paramedics loaded Marisa into the ambulance, and Lucy with her. "Call us from the hospital as soon as you can," Cody told Lucy. She nodded. And then they were gone, leaving Cody standing in the middle of the compound surrounded by bloody towels, feeling drained and stunned.

He looked down at the mess. What was he going to do with three little kids? *Please let them speak better English than their mother, or I'm going to lose it for sure.*

Four

TWO O'CLOCK ALREADY? IT HAD TO BE BECAUSE THERE was the school bus dropping off Shawn at the complex. Cody watched the young man walk across the lot with a bounce in his step, obviously delighted to be out of school for the summer. Cody yearned for the kind of joy Shawn radiated. It had been a long time since he'd felt anything akin to that. So long that Cody wasn't sure if he'd recognize it if it came back into his life.

Bree would recognize it…and help you to do so, too.

He pushed the thought away with a muttered curse. Bree again! She kept invading his thoughts…his heart—

Enough of that. If Bree was going to help him recognize anything, it was trouble. Hadn't she proven that already? *Marisa's fall was as much her fault as mine…*

Even as he thought it, he knew it wasn't true. He wanted to blame her for part of today's disaster, but he couldn't. That was all his fault. No, Bree wasn't responsible. Not for that. But she was responsible for the small, irritating voice that was growing inside him— the voice that kept telling him that Bree's coming into his life promised something much better, if he could be brave enough to reach out and grab hold of it.

He rubbed a hand over his tired eyes. Maybe that was true. He didn't know. But right now she still just felt like trouble on legs.

There was less spring in Shawn's step as he got closer to where Cody was working. He could obviously see the signs of the disaster. "What's up?" Shawn came to a halt in front of him. "This doesn't look so good." He motioned toward the spot where Cody was still trying to patch the banister that Marisa had plunged through hours before.

"It isn't good." Cody raked his hand through his hair. "We had big-time trouble." He told Shawn about the accident. It pained him to do so, watching the boy's light mood disappear before his eyes. "I could use some help from you, Shawn."

"Sure, anything."

Pride in his son swelled in Cody's chest. There may have been moments of trouble in their relationship, but the young man was turning into a fine, dependable guy.

And right now Cody needed that kind of help more than anything else. "Go to Faith Hospital in Fort Myers, where they took Marisa, and find Lucy. See if she can come back with you to pick up Marisa's kids from day care and bring them back here."

Shawn's eyes widened. Well, the kid was growing up, wasn't he? Now was as good a time as any to give him some more adult responsibilities.

Shawn nodded slowly, and Cody thought he stood a little taller. "Will do. Is there gas in the truck?"

"There'd better be. You would know more about that than I would, having been the last one driving it," Cody told him, suppressing the first smile he'd been tempted by all afternoon. Shawn might be responsible, but he was still a seventeen-year-old boy.

"Yeah, well, let me stop by the house; then I'll get going," Shawn said. "Should I bring the phone in case we need to talk?"

Cody suppressed another grin. The translation of that statement to plain, parental English meant Shawn wasn't sure he'd left enough gas in the truck and wanted to go get some cash so that he could fix that little problem as soon as he crossed the causeway. And letting him have the cellular phone would be a clear bonus—one that guaranteed at least one call to his best friend, saying, "Guess what I'm doing this afternoon?"

Cody shrugged. "Sure. Take the phone. But leave it

on and free most of the time so we can get hold of you if anything changes, okay?"

"Will do. See you before dinner, Dad." It was balm to Cody's wounded spirit to hear Shawn call him dad just now. He watched the boy stride across the pavement, no longer bouncing but with a purpose to his steps. At least Cody wasn't a total failure at life. He may have made a mistake that ended in injury for Marisa, but he was still doing some things right.

Cody went back to fixing the banister. Feeling sorry for himself or beating himself up wasn't going to help anybody. Fixing the banister would help. Sending Shawn to get the kids and Lucy would help. One step at a time, he could work his way out of the despair he felt over the situation.

But the most important step involved keeping his mind on his work—and off of Bree Trehearn.

Bree sat in the office, staring at the screen saver in front of her. *I wonder how things are going at the hospital for Marisa and Lucy.* She couldn't shake the feeling that the whole situation had been her fault. If only she had found them and made sure that both Lucy and Marisa had understood instead of relying on a stupid sign that didn't even work, this wouldn't have happened. But no, instead she just let things go, and where had it led? To

Marisa in the hospital and three scared kids waiting somewhere for a mother who wasn't going to pick them up at the end of the day.

Charlotte rose from her chair, looking out the window. "Good. Cody seems to have sent Shawn on a mission. I knew he would, once that boy got home from school." She pointed out the front windows, where they saw Shawn get into the truck, wave at his father, and drive off.

"Is he going to the hospital, do you think?" Bree asked. "I wish I had thought to go out there. I could have gone with him."

"It wouldn't work. There's only room in that truck for three or four people, and Shawn's going to have to get five in it by my count, even if three of them are small children."

"True. I hadn't thought about that part. I just wanted to be there when they went to get the children."

"I know you did." Charlotte came over to where Bree sat and hugged her around the shoulders. "You feel responsible for this somehow, don't you?"

"Of course." Bree looked up at her. "If I had found them the first time I looked, they wouldn't have gone up the stairs with that cart, and Marisa wouldn't have fallen through the railing."

"Bree, where were you four days ago?" Charlotte glanced over the rim of her half glasses, which she'd put on while she reviewed accounts.

"Indiana. No, about halfway through Kentucky."

"And had you ever heard of Island Breeze or Sanibel Island before?"

"Well, no." *Where was Charlotte going with this?*

"Then how can you possibly feel responsible for this accident? It's one of God's little miracles that you're here at all. Don't take everybody's problems on yourself the moment you get here, okay?" Charlotte patted her shoulders.

"Okay. I still feel I was led down here for a purpose, and I can't help feeling like I failed."

"I have no doubt you're here right now for a reason." Charlotte slipped her half glasses off her nose and let them dangle on the chain around her neck. "But I'm not about to second-guess the Lord on what that reason is."

"And I shouldn't either," Bree said softly. But Bree didn't have to second-guess anybody on the reason she was here. She knew why she'd made this crazy trip. It was time somebody else knew, too. Even as Bree pushed the thought away, she knew it was true. Charlotte or Cody should know the reasons for her rapid flight from Indiana.

Panic rose in her chest at the thought of telling Cody. She already looked like a total incompetent to him. Telling him about Bo would be the last straw. No, this was definitely not the time. Not if she wanted to stay at Island Breeze.

"It's hard not to second-guess God sometimes," Charlotte said, watching her with sympathetic eyes. "Now how about getting up and doing something that has no connection to this office or that computer? You could use a break."

"All right." Bree sighed. "I think I'll do that. I'll go back to the apartment, change into some shorts, and walk up the shore for a ways."

"Good idea. But don't forget sunscreen. And a hat, if you have one. And a little bit of bug repellent. Don't want you coming back polka-dotted."

"Yes, mother," Bree muttered, but she didn't mind. Not really. When was the last time someone actually cared about her like this? Bree couldn't remember. And she had to admit, it felt good.

After a few moments Bree was on the beach marveling at her own blindness and stupidity. She had been here four whole days and it had taken near disaster to get her down here to where the sand met the water.

"See, see, see," the seagulls called, wheeling above her.

She looked up, squinting into the bright afternoon sun. The breeze was stiff enough that she had to put one hand on her head to keep her floppy straw hat on. "I see already," she called to the gulls, heedless of who else heard her. Of course, it had taken deep despair for her to see what had been here all along.

The beach and the sun and the wonderful sound of the waves rolling in had been here the whole time. Why hadn't she been down here every day, walking, breathing, praying? This beach smelled different from anywhere she'd ever been in her life. It had as much in common with her rural lane in Indiana as the surface of the moon. It was wonderful.

Her shoes were already off. The sand was smooth under her feet unless she walked to the water's edge. There thousands of little shells crinkled, making the sand and water shift. Bree felt like dancing. For the first time she understood that part of Exodus when Miriam, Moses' sister, danced and sang on the shore with the women.

Of course part of Miriam's jubilation was because Pharaoh's troops were all drowned and the Israelites wouldn't be going back to Egypt—but surely another part had to be the wonder of God's creation here on the sand. Just moments ago Bree been wondering why she was here in this magical place. Now she knew.

"See, see, see," the gulls cried. *See the wonder of my creation,* they sang to her soul, *and know that I am God.*

Cody was still at work on the landing railing when Charlotte found him. She had a tall plastic glass in her hand. "C'mon, boss, break time. Cold lemonade."

Cody wiped sweat off his forehead with one arm. "Gotta get this finished. I don't have time for anything else."

"You don't have time not to." Charlotte handed him the drink. Cold beads of moisture covered the outside of the cup. Taking it from her hand was like walking into a desert oasis. Five swallows and there was nothing in the glass but ice. "Better?" Charlotte grinned knowingly.

"A little." A cold drink did make him feel better. But he knew Charlotte had more in store for him than that. She looked determined. "Now what?"

"Now you put down these tools and go walk on the beach."

"You've got to be kidding." There was no way he was going to do that.

"Dead serious," Charlotte said. "You need to go talk to Bree. In fact, you need to go apologize to her, and that's where she is."

"Apologize? For what?" Was his newest employee really that sensitive? What had he done now?

"She seems to think what happened with Marisa is all her fault. And I know she feels that way in part because of what you said to her. She's really hurting, Cody. Just go and talk to her—five minutes, okay?"

Could anybody say no to Charlotte? Cody didn't

think so. She was a force to be reckoned with. She was also virtually always right in matters concerning people and their feelings. And since Cody was virtually never right on that score, he would bow to her judgment.

"Five minutes." Cody put the glass down on the landing. "Okay." Putting on his sunglasses, he went between the buildings to the wooden sidewalk through the sea oats. How long had it been since he'd walked this stretch of beach? Too long.

While he walked, he thought about Bree. He didn't want her hurting, didn't want her feeling the kind of guilt he felt right now. She didn't deserve that. He found her a little way down the beach. She was different somehow. The dullness that Marisa's accident had brought on her was gone, replaced by a curious kind of glow.

Of course, it could be just a little bit of sunburn. The floppy hat she wore protected most of her, but her hair was blown wild around her face, long silver-gold strands teasing her neck. And the tip of her nose was definitely going to be red soon. It made him want to trace a finger down that sweet spot—

Get a grip, North. You're here for a reason, and touching the lady's nose—or any part of her—ain't it.

"Hi," she said when she saw him, sounding surprised. "I didn't think you'd come looking for me."

It was on the tip of his tongue to tell her that

Charlotte had made him. Instead he went on the offensive a little. "You don't have that fuzzball with you, do you?"

"Gabe? He wouldn't want to be down here. Too hot, too wet, too everything. He would like chasing seagulls, though. And hermit crabs," she said with a giggle. "No, I'm alone."

Bree was almost skipping. Her shoes were off, in one hand. "Don't you take your shoes off? I love feeling the sand." She turned around to face him, walking backward.

"Nah. Just more bait for the sand fleas that way." Cody felt old and jaded. Still, it lifted his heart just to be out here watching her discover the beach. It had been so long since he'd seen it through fresh eyes.

"How long have you lived here?" Bree raised her face to the sky. "Do you come down here every day?"

"Three years full time. And no, not really. At least not just to walk or swim or anything. Most of the time if I'm down here it's to check that nobody's been messing with the sea oats. They're protected. Or to remind kids that bonfires down here are illegal. Or to chase somebody in an ATV off."

"Still the policeman." Bree made a face. It made her look even more like a teenager. A very appealing teenager, he had to admit.

"I guess so. Just with no power to back me up."

Cody picked up a piece of driftwood and pitched it far out past the surf.

"Oh, you've got plenty of power to back you up." Bree danced backward again. "In fact, if you'd just call on it, you could have more power than you ever thought possible."

"Don't go there, Bree," Cody ground out between clenched teeth. "We are not going to have this discussion. If you want to witness about your awesome God to somebody, do it someplace else. Tell Shawn, or Charlotte, or anybody. But leave me out of it."

"I can't leave you out of it," Bree said, lower lip jutting out just a little. "You're one of God's children whether you want to be or not. Why do I get the feeling you weren't always this distant? Why don't you want to talk about it?"

"Let's just say God and I aren't on speaking terms," Cody said. "We haven't been for nearly five years."

"Since before you moved here. What happened?"

"Nothing. That was the problem. My partner and best friend died. And nothing happened. I prayed, I raged, I did everything I knew how, but nothing happened. No answers, no peace, no sense of where I was anymore with God. So I figured, fine, if that was the way he wanted it, that was fine with me."

Bree's face had clouded over. "I'm pretty sure that's not the way he wants anything, Cody."

"Well, fine, Ms. Trehearn. When you have an answer for me, come back and tell me that again. When you can tell me why that awesome, wonderful God of yours just stands by and lets stuff like today happen, why an innocent woman is suffering and in pain, let me know. Or why my fifty-two-year-old partner died out of the clear blue with so many things left to be done, so much life he hadn't lived, you give me an answer. But until then, witness somewhere else, okay?"

Bree didn't answer him. She didn't stop him either when he headed back toward the walkway to his project. She did silently follow him and help with the rebuilding. That meant more than Cody could tell her. Some stubborn will inside him refused to be the first to break the silence, except to request tools.

In fact, it was forty-five minutes before he heard another word out of Bree as they worked together on the landing. Cody alternated between feeling as if he'd slapped a small child and marveling in the weight that was gone from his chest after opening himself to Bree. Still, it wasn't anything he intended to do again in the near future. Of that she could be assured.

Five

BREE FELT DELUGED BY RELIEF WHEN THE TRUCK PULLED up in the parking lot of Island Breeze. She couldn't think of a time when she was as glad to see a particular human being, or in this case, five of them. Lucy and Shawn got out of the truck; then the children piled out.

They looked a little intimidated by the strangers who surrounded them, especially the youngest girl, who drew back a little when Cody came up to where they were standing.

The child was very young. Bree's heart went out to her. She couldn't be more than three, much too young to understand what was going on. One moment her life was normal, and the next she was surrounded by strangers in a strange place.

Knowing all this, Bree was amazed the little girl

wasn't having a full-fledged tantrum. Instead she stood on solid legs, clutching the skirt of her sister's denim jumper for dear life. But she wasn't crying. "It's okay, Sarita," the older girl told her while stroking her hair. "These are the people Tia Lucy told us about, who are going to take care of us until Mama gets out of the hospital."

"I want Mama." The little one's eyes filled with tears.

Lucy stooped down next to the small girl. Her answer, part in English and part in Spanish, seemed to calm the child. Sarita nodded and smiled just a little when Lucy stroked her dark curly hair. Lucy straightened up and turned to Cody and Bree.

"This is Ana. She's nine." She put a hand on the oldest girl's shoulder. Bree thought that she looked old for nine. Not grown-up, particularly, just…old. Like a nine-year-old who spent a lot of time being a miniature grown-up. "Sarita is three. And Carlos, the big boy in the middle, is five."

"I'm six!"

Bree liked Carlos already. He might be loud, and his face was knit into a scowl right now, but Bree could remember making that same face as a child, mainly to convince people she was tough and resilient when she really felt scared inside.

"Not until next week, you're not," his big sister

said, with the authority that only big sisters can manage. Bree smiled.

"You still have to wait a whole week, huh? Birthdays are hard to wait for." Bree ruffled his hair.

"Can we go see Mama? Can she come home with us?" Carlos's dark eyes were liquid. Bree's heart broke.

"Not today, Carlos." Bree automatically went down on her knees. At that level she and the somber-faced boy were almost eye to eye. His eyes were even darker brown than either of his sisters', and Bree could tell he was trying hard not to let his lip tremble. She spoke gently, making her tone as soothing as she could. "But tomorrow we can go see her. And when the doctor says she can come home, we'll get her, okay?"

Lucy looked troubled. "Should you tell him that? I haven't told them much, only that their mama had to go to the hospital to get fixed up."

Bree shrugged. "I don't believe in lying to kids when the truth will do. Sarita won't understand any of this, but the others will. Ana will help us out, won't you?" Bree stood up.

The child's thin shoulders squared. "Sure. I could take care of these kids by myself anyway. I keep telling Mama that. She doesn't need to spend so much on day care, especially now that I'm out of school for the summer. But she says we have to keep going every day while she's at work."

81

"And she's right," Cody snapped. "Nine isn't old enough to be in charge of little kids yet." Bree wanted to tell him that he sounded much sterner than he probably intended. Coupled with his height, towering over all the kids and even the other adults, and the intensity of his gaze, his words sounded harsh. She didn't have time to warn him of that before Ana's tough exterior crumbled and a tear coursed down her cheek.

Cody looked as if he wanted to swear. Bree was sure he was capable of some pretty stiff language, but he was obviously holding back mightily in front of the children. There was suddenly a vulnerability about him that made Bree's heart go out to him. He didn't seem to like making little girls cry. Cody looked at all three unhappy children, and then at Bree. "Help me out here," he whispered.

Bree shook her head. "Can't. I'm in over my head myself."

When Cody spoke, his voice was a little strangled. "I haven't been a dad all that long. I didn't get Shawn until he was twelve. There's a lot of difference between a twelve-year-old boy and younger kids. I didn't mean to bark at you, Ana. I just wanted to tell you that we'd look out for you, that you didn't have to do it yourself."

"Oh." Ana backhanded the tears off her thin face. Bree noticed that her fingernails were painted a coral that was almost orange, and she was glad that Ana still had a few moments sometime to be a little girl. "I thought I was in trouble. Are you sure Mama's in the hospital?"

"Positive." Cody nodded.

"La immigración didn't come get her and you're just being nice to us?" Her narrowed eyes looked much older than nine.

"You heard Bree," Lucy said. "She doesn't lie to kids. And I saw your mama in the hospital. She's going to have a big cast on when you see her tomorrow, but she is for sure in the hospital, not in trouble with immigration."

Bree made a mental note to ask Lucy sometime when they were alone why the child was concerned with immigration. If she could help Ana with at least one of her concerns, Bree would feel better.

As it was, Ana looked relieved just hearing what Lucy had to say. "Okay." Ana relaxed a little. "Now can we have something to eat? And we need to show Sarita where the potty is before something happens."

That got Cody moving quickly. Bree had to stifle a giggle as he sprang into action. "Let's do that fast. We don't want anything to happen like that, at least right away. And once you guys have had time to, uh, wash your hands and stuff, Bree will introduce you to the angel Gabriel."

Bree snorted, taking Carlos by the hand. "Gabriel

is no angel. He's a big white cat with blue eyes. And he likes little kids, especially ones who come to feed him dinner."

"C'mon, Sarita." Ana tugged on her sister's hand. "Let's go. We can see a kitty. *Un gato.* Come on." The parade moved toward Cody's house. Bree wondered where they were going to put these three.

Cody looked at his hall bathroom. It was never going to be the same again. How could three little kids make that much mess just using it once for its intended purpose? There were towels on the floor, the tissue box was empty, and a shiny thread of liquid soap curled all the way around the sink. What would happen at bath time? He shuddered at the thought.

In the kitchen he could hear Bree and the kids. They seemed to be fixing peanut butter and jelly sandwiches. Cody hoped Bree wasn't giving anybody sharp knives to make their own sandwiches. He still wasn't sure how responsible this young woman was. Sometimes she looked like the queen of the space cadets, hair flowing out in all directions, eyes wide, definitely on another planet. But he'd gotten a glimpse of another Bree several times in the last twenty-four hours.

There was a Bree who knew exactly what she was

talking about. This other side of Bree could speak languages that were as foreign to him as Swahili but had to do with disk drives and Internet access. That Bree could also pray in a way that touched him in ways he didn't understand—or, more to the point, that he didn't want to understand. He had to admit it, Bree could be capable and on top of things when she needed to be.

Then there was that laughing, gentle-hearted, completely alluring side of the woman. Even at her spaciest, Bree was beautiful. She moved something deep inside him, a place no one had touched in so very long. She disturbed him and at the same time eased a part of him...it made Cody twitch just to think about all the ways she affected him.

He still wasn't sure of her sandwich-making abilities, though, so after giving the bathroom a quick swipe, he hurried into the kitchen. It wouldn't hurt to see which side of his enchanting young guest was in charge of snack time.

Naturally when he got to the kitchen, Cody discovered that both sides of Bree were involved in snack making. The kids were making their own peanut butter sandwiches and there were containers of raisins, banana slices, and shredded carrot out on the table for decoration.

Thankfully, nobody had any sharp objects. Ana was using a butter knife with a dull edge, Carlos had a frosting spatula, and Sarita had a wooden spoon she was happily pulling in and out of the jar of peanut butter, delighting in the slurping sound she made with every pull.

Bree had a sheepish look on her face when she glanced up to see Cody enter the kitchen. "I know, it's a little bit of a mess. But I figured it might take everybody's mind off a rough day."

"I don't mind messes for a good cause," Cody said. "Hey, Ana, can you help me out for a minute? Keep making your sandwich, just answer a question or two while you make it, okay?"

"I'll try." Ana patted a raisin face onto the peanut butter and sprinkled carrot hair around the edges.

"How does everybody sleep at home? Does Sarita have a baby bed or anything?"

Carlos laughed out loud. "Baby bed! Man, she's three years old. She doesn't sleep in no baby bed."

"Well, some people still sleep in a crib when they're three, Carlos," Bree said softly. "And if Sarita did, we would need to find a way to keep her from falling out of bed."

"Oh. Rita doesn't ever fall out," Carlos said confidently, squashing a lid on his sandwich. "She isn't sleeping with me, though, 'cause she may not fall out of bed, but she sure wets it sometimes."

Before Cody could get any closer to the table, mayhem erupted. The wooden spoon that Sarita was using landed with a resounding thump in Carlos's hair. Peanut butter flew everywhere. "You are bad!" Sarita scolded her brother loudly. "No say that!"

"It may be a long night," Cody told Bree over the heads of the children.

"*May* be?" Bree lifted one eyebrow. "What doubt do you have?"

"None." Cody sighed, separating the warring kids and grabbing a towel to start cleaning Carlos's hair and face. "But I thought for a change I'd be optimistic."

"That was nice of you." Bree's eyes sparkled. "Somebody ought to be. After this little fracas, I don't think Gabe will come down from the top of the refrigerator until morning."

Cody went to wash Carlos while Bree talked to Rita, using Ana to interpret when needed. Walking down the hall to the bathroom Cody had to hold back laughter. "Peanut butter is for eating. Not for hitting your brother in the head," he could hear Bree saying. Funny, nobody had ever had to use that line at his table before Ms. Trehearn came to town. Somehow Cody knew that was no coincidence.

Bree was so tired even her hair hurt. She pushed it away from her face and contemplated the room before her.

None of the kids wanted to sleep in the sleeping bags Cody had at his house. Once they'd met Gabe and seen Bree's sofa bed, all three of them insisted that there was no "cooler" place to sleep in all of the Island Breeze complex than that foldout unit.

Cody protested, telling them they had to come back to the house and sleep. When Bree saw all three of the children start tearing up again, she pulled Cody aside. "Why not let them sleep here?" she asked softly, out of their hearing. She knew enough about children not to give them hope of dividing the adults. "We can go across the way and get their pajamas, then all come back here. It will be fun. If it makes their first night here easier, why not go along?"

Cody's wide brow furrowed. "I hadn't thought of it that way. Are you up to three kids? And where will you sleep?"

Bree was touched that he was concerned for her. "That's not a problem. I worked my way through school being a part-time nanny for one of my college professors. So I'm used to kids. And Gabe and I can pile up the sofa cushions on the floor and take one of those sleeping bags the kids won't use. Really, it'll be fun, like a camp-out."

Cody shook his head. "If you say so. Okay, everybody, Auntie Bree says you can sleep in her bed. If you're going to do that, I want pj's on, teeth brushed, and everybody back over here by eight-thirty, okay?"

"Okay!" Carlos jumped up. "I get to use the bath-room first. And what's pj's?"

"Pajamas," Cody explained. "You have any?"

Carlos shook his head, looking disdainful. "Naw. I sleep in an old shirt of my papa's. He left it when he went to heaven."

Bree exchanged a look with Cody. He seemed as surprised as she was. "Your dad's in heaven?"

Carlos nodded. "Yep. Mama said he went to Sarasota, but I know better. If he went to Sarasota, he would have come back for us by now. I'm pretty sure he went to heaven, 'cause you can't come back from there."

Cody shrugged. Only Bree could hear him as he leaned in to talk to her. "This hasn't come up before. I didn't even know Marisa had three kids until she showed you their picture."

Pulling away from her, he spoke to Carlos again. "Well, go get your shirt, then. And brush those teeth."

"Sure." Carlos scooted off. "I get first dibs on tooth-paste before Sarita squeezes it to death."

His sister's squeal of anger said it all. "Well, looks like we're off to the races again." Cody sighed. "Why do I feel like a greyhound in the middle of the pack?"

All three children were finally asleep. Bree wasn't sure that was ever going to happen until suddenly it did. It was good hearing their even breathing. She'd forgotten how hard it was to cope with this full-time.

Bree felt drained in a way she hadn't in a long time. She had to do something familiar, something she knew how to do. Anything that would make her feel like a competent, functioning human being for a while.

It was late and quiet and Bree yearned for the familiar routine of working with her computer. Just this once she was going to sneak onto the Internet and visit with her cyberbuddies. One quick session couldn't hurt, could it?

Bree padded barefoot to the door that separated her quarters from the office. Opening the door quietly, she tiptoed inside, leaving the door ajar so that she could hear anything that happened in the apartment.

She didn't turn on any lights. No sense doing anything that might wake anybody up. It had taken so long for them to settle down to sleep, she didn't want to do that twice.

Sitting in her desk chair with the computer on, she felt whole in a way she hadn't in weeks. "Just a few minutes," she whispered. "No one's going to know where I am." The glow of the screen felt as welcome as the sunshine on the beach had the last few days.

He had a hit. Bo looked at the screen, very happy that the money he'd paid the little cybergeek from the community college had paid off. Just when he had nearly given up finding her online, Bree had surfaced.

Of course he didn't know exactly where she was. Even Scooter couldn't rig up something that showed him that quickly. It had to be the United States from what was showing up on the screen thanks to Scooter's tracer. But that left a lot of territory. "We can narrow it down," he told the screen on his computer. "And when we do, watch out, Bree. Because I'm coming to find you."

Six

BREE WOKE TO A COOL, MOIST NOSE PUSHING UP AGAINST her nose and cheeks. It was Gabe, up to his morning routine. She blinked and glanced around. She'd really expected one of the children to wake her. Once she'd gotten off the computer she spent a fitful night listening to their sleeping noises and getting up more than once to check on them. She found herself wondering if mothers developed some sixth sense of when to check on a sleeping child and when to leave everything in God's hands.

She had no doubts on how to be a mom to Gabriel, though, and that meant getting up and feeding him when he started butting heads with her in the morning. She opened her eyes, enjoying his bright blue ones surrounded by a halo of feathery white fur.

From her nest of sofa cushions and sleeping bag she could hear giggles coming from the bed. It was Sarita, who was sitting up with one hand covering her mouth. "Are you laughing at the kitty?" Bree asked.

Sarita nodded. "He's funny."

Bree stroked his head, enjoying his full-throated motorboat purr. "He does this every morning. It's his way of telling me he wants breakfast."

"Can I help feed him?"

"Sure. Go to the bathroom and wash your hands first." Bree stroked Gabe's head. "Sneak out of bed quietly so you don't wake Carlos and Ana." Both of the older two still lay flat on the bed. In sleep Ana looked more childlike, arms splayed out and hair rumpled. Bree didn't want her disturbed any earlier than necessary.

"Okay." Sarita slid out from under the covers and somehow got herself to the foot of the sofa bed without touching either her brother or sister, for which Bree was thankful. She bounded into the next room while Bree picked up the cat and held him above her body for a moment, going nose to nose with him again.

"So how are you this morning, Gabe?" She yawned. "Confused by all this commotion?" For an answer he reached out a soft paw and touched her cheek. "I love you too, guy." She settled him on her chest and sat up so that he slid into her lap. He was content to sit there a moment, still purring, while Bree yawned and

94

rubbed her eyes. Then Gabe hopped down and she got up herself, stretching. She still wasn't quite used to the brightness of these Florida mornings.

Dawn was bright in Indiana, but it had never been quite like this. The high windows at the peaked gable of the building let in flashing light that must have danced off the ocean. Patches of it sparkled on the ceiling. There was a clarity to daybreak here that was missing in the landlocked north.

Sarita came out of the bathroom, shaking droplets of water off her hands. Bree grinned. "Couldn't find the towel?"

The little girl shook her head and wiped off her wet hands on Bree's T-shirt. It fit Sarita like a nightshirt, almost down to her ankles. Bree wanted to admonish Sarita not to wipe her hands on her clothes, especially when she was wearing someone else's shirt. But being with Sarita reminded Bree what it was like to be three, and she stifled a giggle instead. "We feed Gabe now?" Sarita asked.

"Yes, we feed Gabe now. Come help me," Bree said, enjoying the child's progress across the carpet on chubby pale brown feet. She virtually danced when she walked, skipping happily as she went into the kitchen portion of the room. Bree pulled a chair over to the countertop, positioning it firmly with the back against the cabinets.

"Here. Stand on this and hold on tight." Bree took the lid off the bin of dry cat food. "Now take this scoop and fill it with Gabe's food. I'll bring over his dish, and you can pour it in. Then we call him. Say, 'kitty, kitty, kitty.'"

"Kee-kee-kee," Sarita chimed as she poured the food. Most of it landed in Gabe's bowl, the sound of which was all the summoning he really needed. He hurried over to the kitchenette and bounded up onto the countertop, much to Sarita's delight. "Breakfast, kitty!" she said. "Is that cereal?"

"No, not exactly. Not the kind you would like, anyway. Should we see if we have some little girl cereal instead of Gabe's cat food?"

Sarita nodded. "And milk. And juice. I'm hungry."

She probably was, Bree thought. None of the kids had eaten much dinner last night, and who could blame them. Being in a strange place with strange people didn't exactly stir up one's appetite. Sarita was rebounding quickly, though.

The little girl glanced up at her. "Have cereal, then go see Mama?" She cocked her head sideways in a charming way that made Bree sure no one refused Sarita much. Not if she was always this cute, anyway.

"First we'll have breakfast and do some things around here for a while. Then we'll call the hospital and see if the doctor will let Mama see you. The doctor has to say it's okay before we can go."

"Doctor? Mama sick?" Sarita frowned.

"Mama has a hurt leg. But the doctor is fixing it, and we can ask Jesus to help make Mama all better very soon."

"Very, very soon. Now." Sarita looked up at Bree with trusting brown eyes and put her hands into Bree's. It pained Bree not to have all the answers for the child. Of course she didn't even have all the answers to her own problems, but that bothered her less. Maybe she needed to ask Jesus for something herself. She needed to ask for faith as childlike as Sarita's, where she could put all her problems on God and expect the solutions very, very soon. Now.

"Let's do that, and then we'll have some breakfast, okay?" Bree gathered Sarita's sweet hands in hers for a quick prayer. Sarita was right. The day would go better if they prayed first, then ate breakfast.

Cody was just finishing up loading the breakfast dishes in the dishwasher when there was a knock on the back door. "Good morning," Bree called out, looking cheerful when he opened the door.

She looked far more cheerful than Cody had expected after a night with three small children. Of course, some of that probably had to do with the fact that Bree seemed to be a morning person. Cody wasn't sure whether to envy her or pity her for that. It certainly made her look fresh and perky first thing in the morning when he was still getting his engine started.

Her hair was combed and arranged, and all of the kids had shiny clean faces with smiles on them. "I guess you guys are ready for breakfast, huh?" Cody said as they trooped into the kitchen.

"Oh, we're ahead of you on that one, Mr. North." Bree smiled. "We've all had cereal and toast and brushed our teeth and are ready to face the day."

"Gabe had cereal too," Sarita told him. "But he didn't brush his teeth. He washed his face."

Cody had to smile. He lowered himself most of the way down to Sarita's level. "I bet he did wash his face. Gabe does that a lot, doesn't he?"

Sarita nodded, pantomiming the cat licking one paw and rubbing it over his face. "He washed my face too. His tongue tickles."

Cody held back his natural reaction to having a cat wash the baby's face. It wasn't what he'd recommend, but he had to admit the cat and the baby probably both enjoyed it. So he clammed up and watched the kids climb up on his kitchen chairs. "So everybody had breakfast? You too, Miss Bree?"

She grinned just like the kids. "Of course. Frosted sugar flakes are my favorite too."

They probably are. She looked like the kind of person who still bought cereal in bright boxes and maybe even kept the toys inside the package. "Great. Now I have four of you on a sugar high," he muttered.

"You won't have us long," Bree told him. "Not if you'll let me borrow Shawn, anyway. I plan to call the hospital and make sure it's okay, then take everybody over the causeway to see Mama if the doctor agrees."

"Sounds like a good idea. And I guess you will need Shawn at least once, to show you where the hospital is."

"Correct." One corner of her mouth went up in a lopsided grin. "You already know my talent for directions."

"True. Anybody who could manage to get to the farthest tip of the island before they run out of gas and still not know where they are or why they're here probably needs an escort into Fort Myers." Bree looked like she wanted to stick her tongue out at him, but there were three impressionable children around, so she merely shrugged.

"Cute, Cody. Not that I can argue. So, can we borrow Shawn?" At this point Cody would have given her just about anything, including Shawn and the keys to either of his vehicles.

"After you borrow my phone." He pointed to the instrument on the wall. "The hospital number is there on the board with the rest. I doubt you'll be able to go in right away anyway. We could put everybody, including Shawn, to work for about an hour before you all leave."

"Can we really?" Carlos bounded out of his chair. "I can help Shawn. I can help Shawn do anything."

"Okay, buddy, you've got a deal." Cody fought a pang of guilt for not thinking about how eager the child would be to spend time with the older boy. "Let's go get Shawn and find out what he's going to do for a while and see how many helpers he needs. Ana, you want to do something too?"

"Sure. If Rita will let me go without her." Ana was so somber and practical. Cody could hardly wait until he could see her smile. He wondered what it would take to get her to do that. Bree's taking her to see her mother would be a start.

In a few minutes Shawn had been tapped to head the work crew, picking up palm debris and generally policing the complex grounds. Sarita was perfectly happy to stay in the kitchen with Bree while she made her phone calls, and Cody finished up the last of the kitchen cleaning while watching them.

It was fun watching Bree while she was occupied. She wrinkled up her forehead when she concentrated, making her look more serious than usual. And she had a habit of twirling a strand of hair around one slender finger.

Midway into the second phone call she obviously got transferred directly to Marisa. "Now, you're sure you are ready to see the children?" Cody watched her smile and nod. "Yes, they are ready to see you. Tell me how things look so I can tell them first. Yes, mostly for Sarita. Yes, she *is* here and she does know we're talking about her. Of course."

"Rita, there is someone who wants to talk to you." Bree handed the child the phone.

Watching her watch the little girl talk to her mother was even more fun than watching her talk on the phone herself, Cody decided.

Bree's smile of delight was almost as big as Sarita's. She leaned her head down toward the phone, as if getting closer to it would help her to understand the quick prattled mix of Spanish and English that made up Sarita's end of the conversation. At least she understood the *adios* at the end.

"No, Rita, don't hang up the phone. Let me talk to Mama again, all right?" Bree deftly whisked the phone out of Sarita's hand before she had a chance to hang it up. Sarita bounced off her chair and ran over to where Cody stood pouring himself one last cup of coffee. He set down the pot quickly so he wouldn't drip any on the child, who was going to run into his legs full force.

"I talked to Mama!" she said, glee in her voice. "We go see Mama. Soon!"

"Good." Cody lifted her up in the air, making her giggle. She weighed almost nothing at all and she smelled delightful, with a fragrance he couldn't quite place. Baby shampoo? Dave had always told him he'd be a good dad. Maybe Dave had been right.

As Cody put the laughing child on the floor, he straightened up with some surprise. For the first time in months, maybe even years, the memory of Dave and something he said hadn't roused bitter or resentful feelings in him. Maybe it was the positive effect of having Bree around. Perhaps her straightforward relationship with God really *was* having some influence on him.

He looked over to where Bree was wrapping up her conversation and wondered again at the open innocence he saw in her face. A strong urge swept him to tell her how important she was becoming in his life after a few short days—but he had no idea how to do that.

Cody shook his head silently. What was he thinking? He couldn't tell Bree something like that. He barely knew her. Better to focus on what he had to get done today, especially if Shawn was going to be taking everybody to Fort Myers. Still, it was nice to have Bree and Sarita in his kitchen, in his life. Maybe God wasn't so distant after all.

Bree had forgotten just how much she hated hospitals. It didn't take her long to remember. All it took was those elevator doors opening on Marisa Montoya's floor, with a big breeze full of eau de disinfectant, or whatever hospitals were perfumed with, to make her heart pound and her stomach feel queasy.

Shawn and the kids didn't seem to have any such problems. The tall teenager was bounding off the elevator in pursuit of Carlos and Rita. "Hey, guys, hold up. Slow down. You need to hold my hand."

Thank goodness for Shawn. Cody had done a fantastic job with this young man. He was friendly and polite, and good with little kids. They skidded to a stop and grabbed his hands, and Shawn took them with good grace. Bree knew not all seventeen-year-old males would walk down a hospital corridor holding hands with little children.

She made a mental note to tell Shawn how much she appreciated his help sometime when they were alone. Then she headed after them, with Ana following her. Ana seemed to be about as thrilled as Bree to be in the hospital. "You okay?" Bree asked the child, swallowing past her own discomfort.

"I guess." Ana's brown eyes were guarded.

"It's a little scary in here, isn't it?" Bree said. "Not real comfortable. It smells funny and there's lots of noise."

"And lots of people," Ana said, warming to the subject and looking calmer. "And *lots* of rules."

"Mostly for the patients' sake." Bree stroked her head. "Now, remember the main one for your mom."

"No jumping on the bed," Ana said, with an expression that clearly said she was much too old for such things. That expression changed rapidly when they reached the door to her mother's room and Bree could see the girl work hard to restrain herself. Carlos and Rita were already crowded up next to the bed, their mother's uninjured arm around both of them.

Marisa looked small and frail. That was the first thing that struck Bree. The cast on her leg overwhelmed her, and there was still an IV pole attached dripping fluid into her arm. There were deep smudges around her eyes, making her look bruised and tired.

I wish Cody were here with us. It surprised her how quickly she had come to depend on the man for strength. He provided it so well that looking up to him seemed natural. If he had come with them, all it would have taken was one look between them and he would know how scared she was. And after a grimace, he would have had something encouraging to say, maybe even a strong arm around her shoulders.

As it was, Bree was the grown-up in charge here. It wasn't a position she liked at the moment. She took a deep breath and her eyes met Marisa Montoya's. That helped, because she could see the joy of having her children with her suffusing her tired face. It was worth her own feelings of alarm and discomfort to know that she was doing the right thing. Seeing that rush of joy on Marisa's face, Bree heard Jesus... *"And when I was sick, you visited me."* Suddenly she didn't need Cody quite as much. Still, that strong arm would've been nice.

It was one o'clock in the afternoon before Shawn strolled up to where Cody was digging out a dead bush. "That lady is something else," he said with no other introduction.

"Who, Bree?" *What had she done now?* It had to be something pretty tremendous to get a reaction out of a tough teenager like Shawn. But then he was discovering that Bree was capable of some pretty tremendous things on a regular basis.

"Who else?" Shawn ran his hand through his short dark hair. "I thought for a minute while we were in Mrs. Montoya's hospital room that we weren't going to come back with those kids. But I underestimated Bree."

"This sounds like a long story. Go get us two cold sodas out of the office and I'll take a break and you can tell me."

Shawn nodded and loped off. In a moment he was back with a can in each hand. Droplets of moisture had condensed on them during the short trek across the parking lot, proving that it was as hot out as Cody thought it was. He discarded his tools and went to sit on the concrete wall that made up one side of the parking garage under unit 3. The wall was the perfect height for both of them to sit on. Shawn was getting close to his height, Cody noted. His son was going to outstrip him one of these days.

Shawn opened his drink and tipped it back, chugging about half of it with a speed that made Cody's throat burn just watching. "Mrs. Montoya speaks a lot better English than you ever gave her credit for, Dad."

"Oh? How come she won't talk to me, then?"

Shawn seemed reluctant to answer for a minute. "She's scared of you."

Cody felt shock that had nothing to do with the cold liquid he was drinking. "Scared? Of me? Why would she be scared of me?"

"Like you have to ask? Heck, Dad, sometimes I'm scared of you."

"You'd better be. But Marisa sure doesn't need to." Cody felt hurt. He never intended to frighten the staff.

"I don't think it's anything you did. I think it's your being an ex-cop and all. She's only here on a green card, and that Mr. Montoya is in prison."

"I knew about the green card. Can't say I knew about the prison part." It did make Carlos's statement that his daddy was in heaven more interesting. What had Marisa actually told the kids? "Her papers are perfectly in order, at least what she showed me when I hired her. And it really isn't any of our business where her husband is."

"Yeah, I know. I wasn't telling you for that reason. I just thought it had a lot to do with why she was scared of you. Anyway, there was this social worker lady that came in while we were there. She was coming to check up and see what Mrs. Montoya was doing with the kids while she was in the hospital. She was talking about foster homes."

Shawn's face darkened, and Cody knew he was remembering his own stay in a few foster homes. There had been several between his young, alcoholic mother's losing custody of him and Cody's taking him in, first as a foster child and then adopting him when he convinced Shawn's natural mother and the courts that the boy belonged with him.

"Bree convinced her otherwise?"

"Yeah, you should have seen her, Dad. She just started witnessing to the social worker. Then she started talking about you. She even had me in the conversation talking about how good a dad you were and stuff. Between that and the prayer with the social worker lady, she never knew what hit her."

Cody had to stifle a laugh. He could see the scene as Shawn described it. No, the social worker probably never did know what hit her. "Are the kids American citizens?"

"All three of them, born in Louisiana and Florida. Mr. Montoya is a citizen too. It's just Mrs. Montoya who isn't. Ana was getting kind of nervous, sure things were going bad, but Bree explained everything to her real clearly. The social worker lady wasn't happy about that either, but once she heard Bree's little speech about not lying to kids, she calmed down."

The laughter was threatening again. Cody was ready to go see Bree and hear *her* description of all this. It wouldn't be nearly as exciting as Shawn's, he was sure. Bree didn't seem to understand the force of her own unique personality.

"So when is Mrs. Montoya getting out of the hospital?" Cody asked.

"Sunday or Monday. She has a cast that goes almost to her hip. She's going to be in a wheelchair for a while, because it's a...I can't remember what the nurse called it—"

"Nonweight-bearing cast," Cody said, remembering a suspect who'd cleared an eight-foot fence in front of him years ago and cost the county a bundle of money. "Yeah, she's going to be in a wheelchair for a while. And then on crutches after that."

"Yeah, Bree was already making plans. She said if the lower unit was available on building 3 or 4, maybe they could all move in there until Mrs. Montoya got more mobile."

She could have cleared it with me first. But it did make perfect sense. Marisa couldn't handle three kids in whatever small apartment she was probably in now. Not in a wheelchair or on crutches. And he did feel responsible for her anyway. So Bree's idea would work well.

Cody raked his hand through his hair. "Think you can get on the computer and figure out how to shift the paying customers around for a couple weeks so that we won't have to move the Montoyas?"

"Too late. Bree's already doing that; started the minute she got Sarita settled down for a nap with Gabe. When I went to the office to get our drinks, she was talking to some lady in Michigan, telling her about the superior view from Jacaranda's top unit as opposed to Sea Palm's ground floor."

Cody snorted. "She's never been in Jacaranda's top floor."

"No, but she sure has a great imagination." Shawn folded his arms. "By the time she was finished I wanted to move in there myself."

Cody shook his head. "Let's go over there before she gets into too much trouble, shall we?"

Shawn got up off the half wall. "I don't think that's possible, Dad. Bree seems like one of those people who doesn't have to go looking for trouble. It just naturally finds her on its own." For once, Cody couldn't agree more with his son.

Seven

Bree looked around the condo unit, trying to imagine it as home for a family. It wasn't really meant for a permanent home, but it would do. Marisa's wheelchair wouldn't fit every place the way it should, especially in the bathroom. Fortunately the wheelchair would only be for a couple of weeks; then she would graduate to a walking cast and crutches.

Maybe I could talk to Cody about handicapped access. If they had a couple of units that were really accessible to people in wheelchairs, think of what a draw it would be.

"Whoa, girl, you're getting ahead of yourself again." Right now the task at hand was to figure out how to set up the unit to best accommodate Marisa and the kids. She couldn't do anything that couldn't be undone for the next renters, so that left out knocking out walls or repainting one of the bedrooms into something that would be more appealing to the girls.

She wondered if the king-sized bed in the master bedroom was really bolted into the wall unit or if it could be moved. If so, the children could take that room and they could put a hospital bed for Marisa into the smaller second bedroom. *If* the door in there would let a wheelchair through. "So many things to think about, Lord." *And every one distracts you from what you should be doing,* came the answer as clearly as if someone had spoken it. She still hadn't told Cody why she was in Florida. Bree knew that once he found out about why she'd left Indiana with such haste, he was going to be concerned and probably angry.

Probably? Bree corrected herself. Cody would *definitely* be angry. His expression would make the glare he'd given her the first night on the beach look kind. That expression was one of the main reasons keeping her from telling him the truth. Okay, that and the fact that as a former police officer he would want her to call the police in Indiana and settle things there. But she couldn't. Not yet. Doing that would call attention to her here. And she couldn't bear to see that frown return to his face when he looked at her. Not when he was just starting to look at her...differently.

Besides, she was keeping a low profile. Nobody

had any idea she was here. Surely things were safe for a while, long enough for her to get Marisa settled with the kids, anyway. At least that's what Bree told herself. Now, she decided, back to figuring out the layout of this place. She was going to have to find a tape measure, one of those rigid metal kinds that carpenters used. Of course that meant tracking down Cody, but it had to be done.

It was hard not to blurt out her secret when she found him. Bree felt awful deceiving him. *He's a stranger; what does it matter?* The answer came swift and sure: it mattered because she cared about the irascible Cody North and his feelings a little more each day. Lying, even by staying silent, was getting harder and harder.

Still, when Bree found Cody, she didn't blurt out her secret. "I need a tape measure, one of those metal kinds. Do you have one?"

"Of course." Why had she ever doubted that an organized individual like Cody would be without one?

He looked every inch the competent manager today, on the job and working. His khaki cargo shorts had things sticking out of every pocket. It was hard for Bree not to notice that they fit him well, too. His Island Breeze golf shirt had a distinct smudge on one shoulder but looked crisp otherwise. His dark hair was tousled in a way that tempted her fingers to straighten it for him, and his eyes were shaded with his trademark sunglasses.

"What are you going to use this for?" Cody asked, one eyebrow lifted. When he looked at her that way, Bree just wanted to melt.

"Measuring, of course." Bree pushed away her distracting feelings.

"Just measuring? No activity I would worry about afterward, like cutting new doorways in that unit you want to use for Marisa and the kids?"

"Of course not," Bree told him, trying not to sound huffy. "Would I do something like that?"

"Don't know. I haven't figured out enough about you yet to tell. *Would* you do something like that?"

"Not to someone else's property," Bree had to admit. "It would be kind of neat, though, Cody. Have you ever considered making a couple of units handicapped accessible? Think of the crowd you could draw."

"Think of the expense I could incur. And how many people in wheelchairs go to the beach? Sand dunes aren't exactly wheelchair friendly either." He was always so practical, albeit in a negative way. Bree was sure that if she stayed around long enough that would drive her just a little bit crazy. Of course, Cody was already driving her a little bit crazy. His enigmatic smiles, Gary Cooper-like answers, and those wonderful golden eyes—when he didn't have them covered up with sunglasses—were combination enough to send her right over the edge of a small cliff. She had to watch herself around Cody North or things could get difficult.

"Just measuring?" His too-patient tone brought her back to the present.

"Just measuring. I was thinking about switching around the beds so that Marisa could have the smaller room and the three kids the master suite. If everything fits right, that is, including the wheelchair."

Cody smiled. "That's actually a good, practical idea. I'm impressed you thought of it."

"I'm not the queen of the airheads, Cody." Bree tried to contain her aggravation. His expression told her she'd hit a nerve. "It does show, you know. Your belief that I've got cotton candy where most of my gray matter ought to be."

"Not cotton candy, exactly." His face was flushed, making Bree want to giggle. "I'm never quite sure where you're coming from. It's...unsettling."

"I'll bet it is. You like things pretty orderly and logical, don't you?"

"As a rule, I do. And things around you don't tend to stay orderly. Or logical, for that matter. Not in my kind of logic, anyway. Most of what you do has its own kind of logic when I stop and think about it. It's just a brand of logic that doesn't correspond with mine."

"True," Bree said. "Want to help me measure the condo? Maybe we could combine our logics and come up with a plan to get this place set up for Marisa and the kids."

"I think you're quite capable of measuring by yourself. But when it's time to move furniture, come get me. You will need help for that."

"Will do." Bree was out the door and halfway across the crushed shell of the parking lot before she realized she'd been given a compliment. Cody hadn't put down her idea or discounted it in any way. He'd told her to come get him *when* she needed to move furniture, not *if* she needed his help. They were making progress, she decided. There was a spring in her step as she went into the condo.

She'd gotten him again. Every time Cody thought it was safe to be around Bree, he got snagged once more. How did he go from doing necessary chores around the complex—and making good time at them, thank you very much—to moving furniture with a crazy lady? Okay, so not a *crazy* lady, exactly. A lady of definite opinions, most of which didn't match his own.

She was strong for being slender and slight. Cody was impressed by the way she hauled around her end of the mattresses and bed frames they lifted and moved from room to room. And he had to admit her idea worked. The king-sized bed fit in the smaller bedroom along with the chest of drawers that had been there before.

The master suite looked different with a spare double mattress and frame from storage and a twin lined up where the big bed usually was in a normal unit. The nightstand from the smaller bedroom divided the area nicely so that Carlos would have a little space separate from his sisters. "You're okay, Trehearn," Cody heard himself saying. "Ever thought of going into residential design?"

Bree laughed. "I did, actually. Architecture was on my list of possible careers. But school was expensive, and I was on my own by then. No scholarships, since I bounced around a lot. My dad was military and I went to three different high schools. And I guess I didn't have the best grades."

"That's rough. I went to school in the same town from kindergarten through graduation. Had some of the same people in my class all the way, thirteen years."

"Wow. I don't think I ever went thirteen *months* in the same school," Bree said, sounding wistful. "At least I never got too attached to anyplace. It makes moving easier. I can pick up and move in an instant."

"And apparently do." He still wondered how she'd been able to leave an established business in Indiana and just take off the way she apparently had. And why, for that matter, anybody would want to. Still, the more he found out about Bree, the less anything she did surprised him. The lady was nothing if not a free spirit.

Drove him nuts.

"Point taken. I guess what I did looks pretty squirrelly from your perspective." Bree bit her lip.

"Different, at least." Today was going so well that he didn't want to hurt or offend her. "I spent most of my life within fifty miles of Tampa, and went through the academy there and joined the force. You've been everywhere. It has to make for a different perspective on life."

"It probably does. Sometimes God was my only constant. The first thing I did when we moved each time was find a church with an active, Spirit-filled youth group. My parents weren't particularly interested in church, but there was always someplace near the base for me to find a church home."

Cody looked at her again. Bree looked strong and resilient in tan shorts and a sleeveless white top. Still, he could see the lonely teenager she must have been. Maybe not lonely, he corrected himself, but definitely alone except for the Lord. "What's it like? To be that sure of God?"

"What's stopping you from finding out for yourself?"

There was the Bree he'd come to expect. Her blue eyes flashed challenge as she pushed tendrils of pale hair off her neck.

"Nothing, I guess. No, make that everything." This was harder than moving a dozen king-sized mattresses.

"You sound as if you feel you're on the outside looking in, Cody. God doesn't operate that way. That's what Jesus is for, to draw us in and make us children of the King."

"I know, Bree. I even believed it once. It's just that God seems so…I don't know, far away." Were there tears burning his eyes? He hadn't cried since Dave's funeral.

"Something made you feel this way," Bree said. It was a statement of fact, not a question.

The words seemed to flow out of him. Cody couldn't have stopped them if he wanted to…and he wasn't sure he wanted to. No, he didn't talk about this with anyone, but with Bree it felt right. "I knew a man. He was my best friend. My partner. He was a good man and he loved the Lord like nobody else I knew. And he died. He wasn't shot, he didn't drive into an accident; he just went home from work one day and sat in his favorite chair and never got up."

"And you can't understand why a loving God would let that happen." Bree put down her end of the mattress and came to him.

"You've got it. I couldn't understand it then, and I still don't understand it. All I know is it's hard for me to believe in that loving God you talk about who invites us into his circle."

"What if you never understand?" Bree asked. "It may happen that way. Even Jesus said there are things that are beyond our earthly understanding. I don't think we're supposed to let something like that get in the way of our love for God. It doesn't get in the way of his love for us."

"Yeah, but he's God. There's nothing beyond his understanding."

"Do you really have to understand, Cody? Because I can't help you with that. Nobody can except God, and his way of helping may not be your idea of the right way at all."

"Then we're both out of luck, Bree. Because I need some answers I can understand." Cody's voice sounded harsh even to himself, but it was the truth. That loving God Bree talked about didn't sound real to him right now. Maybe he never would.

"I'll pray for you, Cody." She looked as solemn as Ana. She hugged him and he let her, walking into her embrace. It felt good to be there for a moment. He couldn't stay, but for a moment it felt right to let her stand on tiptoes and envelop him.

She felt so good, and smelled even better. Soft and

resilient to the touch, her hair scented with something that was floral and reminiscent of sun and ocean at the same time. Cody rested his cheek on top of her hair for a moment; then he broke the embrace. "You do that, Bree, if it makes you feel better. I can't pray. Haven't in years. I feel like I'm knocking on a door, but nobody's home."

Her eyes were wide and swam with unshed tears. "There's always somebody home in God's house, Cody. Always." And then she went into the next room. Cody gave her a few minutes to get composed, kicking himself the whole time for upsetting her.

"Ready to get the last of this moved?" he asked, trying to show no emotion.

Bree nodded, wiping her face with the back of her hand, reminding him again of a child. "Let's do it. I want everything right when Marisa comes tomorrow. It won't be home, but we'll do our best."

Of that Cody was sure. Bree did her best at everything she set out to do. This project to settle Marisa's little family in their temporary home would be no different. She would do her best, even if it took more strength than she really had. Cody felt a rush of gratitude in his heart that Bree had run out of gas when she did and ended up on his stretch of beach that dark, rainy night.

As much as she aggravated and annoyed him, Bree

Trehearn might be just what he needed to shake things up in his life.

Not that he understood her or anything. He spent the rest of the day trying to figure out if there was a way he could get to know her better, get to know what made her tick, without scaring her off. After dinner— another rather wild affair involving all three children, Shawn, Bree, and himself,—Cody finished cleaning the kitchen while Shawn and Bree loaded the kids into her little car and took them to Pinocchio's for ice-cream cones.

It came to him while he loaded the dishwasher. He could fiddle around with that computer. If anything told him what made Bree do what she did, it would be that piece of machinery. Finishing up in the kitchen, he went across to the office.

It turned on when he tried it, which he took as a good sign. Less of a good sign was its reaction when he pressed the button on the mouse the first time. The thing started talking to him in strange beeps and chirps followed by a hiss. Something about connecting came on the screen, and it sounded like the computer made some kind of telephone connection. Great. What had he done now? Probably phoned Tokyo or something without knowing it.

Cody moved the mouse around, clicking, but couldn't seem to get out of whatever he was in. After a few minutes of trying various things to no avail he shrugged and gave up. He was pretty sure that if he just turned everything off, he could shut down the computer's phone connection to whatever or whomever it was talking to. Hopefully Bree would be none the wiser.

He turned off everything, looking for blinking or glowing buttons. Finally he got to a point where there weren't any. After thirty seconds he picked up the office phone. Cody didn't know when a dial tone had sounded that sweet. Putting down the phone, he shook his head. So much for his "easy" way to get to know Bree. With a sigh, he went back to the house to wait for the ice-cream eaters.

"She's not as smart as you thought," the phone message rasped in Bo's ear. It was nice to see that Scooter valued his contact after all. "She came online again, not twenty-four hours later, from the same location. One more hit and I can figure it out within a few miles for sure, maybe even a few blocks. I can tell you right now it's in the southeast. Georgia, Alabama, maybe Florida. Catch you later."

Good old Scooter. Bo wondered if he would have been as cooperative if he'd known the real reason he was looking for Bree. What Scooter didn't know wouldn't hurt him. It was only if he really found out that there might be hurt involved.

Bo doodled circles on the pad next to the phone. They were getting closer. The circles took on the shape of a target, dark and light circles within each other. "Soon, Bree. Very soon, we'll be hitting the bull's-eye."

Eight

IT DIDN'T LAST LONG. CODY NEVER EXPECTED ANY KIND of happiness to last long, because that just wasn't part of his experience in life. So when the euphoria he felt over knowing Bree a little closer faded by the next day, he wasn't surprised. If he would have thought about how things had gone in the past for him, he could have predicted that he'd come down to earth with a hard thump.

The only thing that surprised him was what brought him back to reality. "Where can we find what?" he found himself asking Bree that morning.

"A piñata and a piñata bat," she said again slowly, as though she were speaking to a dull child. "You know, one of those big papier-mâché things you stuff with toys and candy and all, and the stick you hit it with to break it open so everything falls out."

"Why would we want one?"

"For Carlos's birthday party. See, I thought we could have a party next Wednesday morning with all the kids who are in the complex, and the adults too if they want to come. We could put candy in the piñata, and maybe some gift certificates from other places like the bookstore and one of the shell shops. It would be fun. He'd have a birthday party, which Ana says he's never had before, and the guests would have a good time."

Cody shook his head. "I've never had parties for the guests before, birthday or otherwise."

"Then now is the perfect time to start, Cody. Don't you see, you want people to come back. Repeat business is what things are about down here. I've only been here a week and I've learned that. Do you know that Mel at the bicycle rental place says 75 percent of his business comes from return customers?"

Cody didn't even *know* Mel at the bicycle shop. All right, that was an understatement. He assumed that the guy at the chamber of commerce meetings with the Mel's Island Cycle Shop shirt was Mel, but he had no real confirmation of that, having never talked to him. Still, he couldn't tell Bree that. It would only confirm her opinion of him as a grumpy hermit. "That's no surprise, Bree, but how does a birthday party for Carlos, where we spend my hard-earned money, give us repeat customers?"

"Easy." Bree snapped her fingers. It really sounded easy, the way she said it. Her blue eyes glowed with enthusiasm for her wacky idea. Cody wished he could get her eyes to glow like that for other reasons...like because of him...

He shook off the thought. *Focus, man. Don't even go there.* He forced himself to listen to her bubble on.

"People come to Island Breeze. They have a good time, especially families with kids who want to vacation here again next summer. They remember what a good time they had. They book again here. Maybe they even sign up to have this week permanently."

"Because of a piñata? I don't think so." Cody folded his arms across his chest in a "case closed" gesture. Maybe that would discourage her.

Bree was loaded for bear. Her chin thrust out in that look of determination that was starting to give him hives. "What can it hurt?"

"Besides my finances?" The list was endless. Where did Cody start for this eternal dreamer? "Well, there would be the liability of turning little kids loose with a bat. Blindfolded, I believe, isn't it? What if one of them walks into the pool, or stumbles on a red anthill? Lawsuit city, here we come." He hated to deflate her, but it had to be done. Bree didn't have his experience in business to back up her crazy schemes.

Bree huffed. "You're impossible. You see the worst in every situation."

Cody shook his head. "And you don't see anything because you don't plan ahead. If something sounds like a good idea, you plow ahead in a split second. Somebody's got to put the brakes on for you, sister."

"Why?" She looked like a stubborn child, lower lip starting to pout. Except Cody had never wanted to kiss a child who looked this way. With Bree, it was all he could do not to take her in his arms and kiss her senseless—and that irritated him even more than her ridiculous birthday party idea! "Please, tell me what is so awful about wanting a kid to have a party on his sixth birthday? A little cake and ice cream, some punch, one silly piñata…"

"This is getting more complicated at every step. First it was just the silly piñata," Cody reminded her.

"It would make a better party with the cake and ice cream too." She cocked her head, looking for all the world like her goofy cat when he was watching lizards outside his window. Only Cody knew he was the one about to be pounced on. "What if I said I'd pay for it myself, instead of getting anything out of petty cash? That I'd get everything to stuff the piñata free, and make sure nobody stepped in an anthill or went swimming by accident?"

"I guess," Cody grumbled. How could he possibly refuse her? "We'll try it this once. But if it's a bust, you tell me I was right. And no more goofy stunts."

"Deal!" She gave him a quick hug, making his heart race and making him wonder if a hug from Bree was the real reason he'd said yes. He did like those hugs.

She bounced off to go start planning, and Cody could see the wheels in her head spinning with plans. "I can ask Charlotte about the piñata. I bet she knows where to find one, what with the children's ministries at the church. And the bookstore might give me some of those cute little erasers along with the coupons..."

Hurricane Bree, at it again. How had he let himself get talked into this? Cody stood and watched her plot, plan, and bounce toward the office. This woman was a menace to society. A very attractive menace, but a menace nonetheless. If she stayed another week she'd be running the place, and instead of his well-ordered life the complex would resemble the winter home for Ringling Brothers, complete with elephants, clowns, and ponies.

How could he ever have thought Bree harmless? Her energy level was positively scary, and her enthusiasm would be catching for a weaker soul. He was going to have to find out more about her, definitely. Feeling a sinking sensation around his heart, Cody pulled out his cellular phone. There was no sense going into the office to try to use the regular line. Even if he wanted Bree to hear this call, he couldn't use the phone because she would be calling four counties trying to find a piñata by now.

He flipped open the gray phone and dialed a familiar number. "Hi, let me speak to Harry Howell, please." There was a pause, and then his friend Harry was on the line.

"Hey, Harry. I think you still owe me one for that last abandoned stolen car I found for you on my May bike run. Yeah, I need a favor this time. Run somebody through the computer for me, will ya, a prospective employee, we'll say. Trehearn. Bree. Yes, that's her real name, or at least that's what she claims. White female, date of birth early seventies, about five-seven and 120, maybe 125, last known residence Yorktown, Indiana..."

There was no turning back now. Cody was committed to checking out Bree with the police. He just hoped he got an answer he could live with.

Settling Marisa and the kids into the condo was harder than Bree had imagined. Of course she always looked for the best in everything and was surprised when things didn't work out that way. So the little glitches, like discovering that maneuvering Marisa's wheelchair in the bathroom was like trying to waltz with a giraffe, were major challenges.

"I measured. Twice," Bree said, puzzled. She hadn't counted on the arc the wheelchair had to make turning around to maneuver between the sink and the commode, or the impossible task of getting an adult in a full-leg cast anywhere near the bathtub.

Marisa didn't seem fazed by anything. "This will work. I pray, you pray, we figure something out." Marisa's cheerfulness in the face of these problems amazed Bree. She always thought of herself as a positive person, but the tiny Hispanic woman had her beat by a country mile.

In a wheelchair for four weeks? No problem. Not working and three kids to feed? In broken English and through Ana, Marisa had the answers. *"Dios...* God, he provide, Bree. He give to us you, and Señor Cody, *sí? Mi* Carlos...he not give up the drugs. He go to prison. But me? I put cares on God." She nodded firmly. "God provide all. You will see."

Bree wasn't sure "all" described what she'd found in the tiny apartment the four of them had been subletting in a rough neighborhood in Fort Myers. The kids only had about three changes of clothes, none of them new. Marisa didn't have much more herself. It was all neat and clean, well kept. There just wasn't much there. Most of the furniture had come with the apartment;

Marisa only owned a battered rocking chair and a tiny table in the way of furniture. Two moving boxes held most of the family's possessions. One more plastic crate held the children's toys and books. Moving into the condo wasn't difficult, except for the wheelchair.

Even so... maybe Marisa had a point. The children didn't look like they wanted for anything. They were tickled that their new home had cable TV, a luxury they never had before. Charlotte had promised to bring some kind of videos with giant dancing carrots over from the church to put in the VCR. Sharing a bedroom didn't bother the kids at all, especially when there were two beds in it.

"Carlito is soon too big to share a room with girls. Maybe we find a..." Marisa faltered a little, needing a word she didn't have in English. She called Ana over, and between them they came up with, "Not a wall, Mama. A screen?"

"*Sí*, a screen. For between Carlos and the girls. So he can be alone to play."

"Or get dressed," Ana said. "I don't want to see his underwear, and he doesn't want to see mine."

"Pink Barbie girl stuff," Carlos exclaimed. That said everything.

"I'm sure we can find a screen, or something to block off his part of the room," Bree said. "You're right, Carlos, you are a big boy to share with the girls. And getting bigger, or at least older, very soon. Can we give him a birthday party, Marisa?" Only after she asked did Bree think that she should have done the asking in private so that Marisa could answer without the children watching.

"Maybe. There is not much money. And the hospital will want most of it."

Bree waved her hand in a gesture of dismissal. "Don't worry about the money. I'm finding ways to do this without much. Like you said, God provides. It's easy to trust him about something as simple as a birthday party."

"Good," Marisa said, a smile creasing her face for the first time since she got to her new home. Bree couldn't hold back a responding smile. When Marisa smiled like that, she didn't look much older than Ana.

Bree wondered just how old the tiny woman was. Probably not much past her own twenty-six years, and already with a family to support. It made Bree think. Her problems paled beside Marisa's, and yet the small woman was able to put her trust in the Lord. If God could handle Marisa's overwhelming challenges, he certainly wouldn't have any trouble with Bree's problems. Was it time to go to him with all her problems instead of trying to manage them herself? She didn't feel she was doing the best job.

Staying quiet here at Island Breeze, closed off from

the Internet, not doing what she did best, felt odd. More than odd—it felt wrong. But it was the only way Bree knew to stay hidden from the man who was surely trying to track her down. As long as she stayed hidden and quiet, he couldn't find her. Still, she wasn't getting much accomplished, either. That computer she'd installed in the office mocked her. Charlotte was already clamoring for lessons on how to use it, how to put up an Internet site that would benefit the condo complex and get Cody the bookings he needed to stay afloat.

"After all, we need them more than ever if we're going to support Marisa and the kids," Charlotte said. Bree knew she was right but so far had resisted Charlotte's pleas for training. Still, it was only a matter of time. Could she do what Marisa was doing and boldly put all her troubles on the Lord?

At least the kids kept Bree constantly occupied so that she couldn't mull over the serious questions too long. Right now it was Sarita, springing around her mother's wheelchair, insistent for juice, a story, and having her hair fixed, all at the same time.

"You can climb here for a story. Go get the hairbrush first. Ana or Bree will get you juice," her mother said.

Sarita's lower lip trembled. "Don't want to get the brush. Don't want Bree get my juice. Want Mama to do it. Mama do it all."

134

"Mama cannot do it all, Sarita. Mama needs help. You can help Mama and be a big girl. Now go." Marisa patted her on her rump and sent her on the way to get the brush and juice.

Sarita wouldn't be sent so easily. She flopped into a boneless, wailing pile on the floor. Bree looked at the child and then the mother, unsure what to do.

Marisa shook her head, motioning Bree to leave the child alone. "When she's ready she will come here."

Marisa was right. After a few minutes of wailing, and realizing that no one was paying much attention, Sarita got up. She came over and climbed into her mother's lap in the wheelchair and leaned her head on Marisa's chest. "Don't like being a big girl." She popped a thumb into her mouth.

"Nobody does," Bree told her. If Sarita would have understood, Bree would have told her that even she didn't like being a big girl all the time, especially when it meant owning up to your mistakes.

Marisa laughed. "She is right. Sometimes being big girl is not fun. But Mama is big girl, and Bree is big girl, and Sarita is big girl, too."

"And all of us big girls have work to do," Bree said. "I'll come back in an hour or so and check on you, all right?"

"Fine." Marisa cuddled Sarita. "We will be here."

That was true, Bree reflected on her way out of the

condo. Marisa couldn't go much of anyplace on her own yet. Sarita's temper storm had shown Bree the truth of her convictions, though. It was time to be a big girl herself and tell Cody just why she was here on Sanibel Island. She was going to have to tell the truth even though it meant Cody would be angry with her, which she knew was the case. It was time to face up to things, even if it wasn't any fun.

Even if Cody might make her leave...

In the office Charlotte was working on the computer. "This is so much fun." She smiled as Bree came in. "It's going to make so many things around here a snap. And that solitaire game! How do you take that thing off this machine? Otherwise I'm going to get in a world of trouble."

Bree was about to tell her that solitaire troubles were easily remedied when the telephone rang and she picked it up. "Island Breeze Condos, your vacation home away from home."

The man with a deep voice asked for Cody. When Bree looked at Charlotte and mouthed his name silently she pointed to the closed office door, shaking her head.

"He can't be disturbed right this minute, sir. Can I have him call you back?"

"Is this Charlotte?" Bree didn't have time to correct him before he went on. "This is Harry. Just tell Cody I got the information he was after. Tell him Ms. Trehearn is clean as a whistle, if that is in fact her name. No record I can pull up anyplace, nothing but an Indiana driver's license with no points against it. Looks like a good hire to me."

"Oh. Okay. Thank you," Bree managed to choke out before she put down the phone.

Charlotte turned to Bree. "Message?"

"I'll write it down myself." But her fingers were shaking too hard to hold the pencil and write on the pink notepad in front of her. Cody had called the police about her! All the time she thought he was trusting her, he was checking her out instead.

Bree didn't know what to do. It was one thing to come in here, ready to tell Cody everything. Somehow it didn't feel like such a noble gesture anymore, or even the right thing to do, if he was going to go behind her back and call the police. Why should she help his sneaky little scheme along?

Bree thought back to the day before when Cody's embrace had felt so right. Had he already called his buddy Harry then? Had he been wondering if he were hugging a criminal? Her anger blazed as she put down the pencil. She'd deliver this message herself, but not this minute. If she tried to deliver it now, she'd hiss and spit like Gabe on a bad day.

"I'll be back," Bree told Charlotte. "I need a short walk on the beach." What she really needed was a walk around the entire island, Bree thought as the glass door to the office closed. It would take *that* long just to cool down.

Nine

SHE HAD ACTUALLY BEEN FALLING IN LOVE. BREE NEARLY dropped the piñata when the thought hit her. Before Cody's little trick of checking up on her with his police sources, she had honestly been falling in love with him. How could she have been so foolish? Bree put the piñata on the picnic table and struggled to collect her thoughts.

Wasn't it bad enough that she'd had to leave everything she was comfortable with, everything she knew, because of one man? It was unbelievable she could get involved with another one so quickly. Granted, Cody was worlds away from what Bo had been. And she had never even remotely considered the possibility of a romantic encounter with Bo.

Still, the thought of trusting anybody as much as

she'd begun to trust Cody was scary. Bree couldn't believe she'd actually allowed herself to go that far with her emotions in the short week and a half she'd known Cody North. Maybe this was just a mad crush of some kind that would play itself out if she ignored it. As soon as Bree thought that, she had to admit it wasn't true. Cody appealed to her on basic levels that had nothing to do with a crush.

He was honest. He appeared to be a man with strong convictions, even though he was wrestling with his faith. With Bo the challenge had always been to get him to see that God existed, that there were convictions to be held besides the somewhat warped ones that Bree had taken for a joke when she first met him. Surely nobody believed things as wild as Bo spouted, did they? He was just being outrageous to entertain the kids at the student union at the college.

With Cody it was evident in a moment that he had strong beliefs, and they included treating everyone he came into contact with fairly whenever possible. Bree suspected that such an attitude had probably been hard to keep while being a police officer. Didn't they see the worst of most people? Let's face it, nobody said, "Oh, good, Officer, I'm so happy you stopped me for speeding."

Yet Cody wasn't a total cynic. He dealt fairly with Shawn, loved him as much as Bree could imagine anyone loving their own child however they came to them. He'd taken in Marisa and the kids without a complaint. It was only her whom Cody was checking up on.

Heat filled her face again at that thought. How could Cody do that? How could he have the police checking her out as if she were some kind of criminal? Okay, so they'd met on a dark beach with her running around looking for a cat. And she still couldn't tell Cody where she was, or why she'd gotten there. Add in the fact that she'd shown up in the middle of the night, out of gas, all her worldly belongings in her car...obviously frightened...more than likely looking for all the world like she was on the run....

Bree bit her lip. Maybe Cody had some cause for concern. Actually, in his eyes, probably a *lot* of cause. She supposed it wasn't any surprise he decided to check up on her. Bree might have done the same if her first introduction to Cody had been running around in the soybean fields near her house in Indiana. Especially in the middle of the night under strange circumstances.

Maybe she shouldn't be angry. In fact, maybe it was time she admitted to herself that she had some major confessing to do. She needed to confess both to God and Cody her anger, her resentment, and the things she'd been hiding.

At least she'd only been hiding them from Cody. Bree knew she couldn't hide anything from God.

Confessing there would be comfortable and familiar. Not easy, perhaps, but an experience she had often. And Bree knew that God forgave her already. It was Cody she wasn't so sure about. She suspected that confessing anything to him would be anything but comfortable.

Which was why she was working on hanging the piñata while she talked to God instead of finding Cody. She was putting up the last of the streamers and planning to go look for her somewhat severe boss when Carlos bounced onto the grass.

"I'm six, Bree. Really six today!"

"I know. Are you ready to have a party to celebrate?"

Carlos nodded vigorously. The little boy gleamed. His dark hair shone and his white T-shirt looked as if it could glow in the dark. Bree wondered how long that would last. Wasn't chocolate cake the natural enemy of a white shirt? And those bright blue icing flowers were going to show up beautifully on Carlos.

Bree grinned wide enough to match the excited little boy. "Does Mama need some help getting to the party?"

His smile wavered. "She says she's not coming. It's too hard to get here."

"I don't think so, Carlos. We'll just have to look for Super Shawn and the crew. They can get her here, no

142

problem. Let's go find them, okay?"

"Okay!" Carlos smiled even wider than before, a feat Bree would have said was impossible a few minutes earlier. She breathed a quick prayer, hoping this would be as easy for Shawn and the rest of the grounds crew as she promised. Of course being strapping teenagers, they'd make it look easy even if it nearly killed them.

Bree headed out, following Carlos. He bounced up the path, calling loudly for his buddy Shawn. Bree wished she could be that carefree about life.

So what's stopping you? a small voice challenged.

Nothing but fear. Fear of the future. Fear of the truth.

Cody looked around at the pool area. Everybody was having fun. They were really enjoying themselves. A group from Michigan who came every summer was talking to Marisa and Carlos. Cody hadn't ever seen them talk to anybody before. The man was laughing, and seeing that was another first for Cody. He was going to have to eat his words to Bree.

Don't you just hate it when that happens? Dave's favorite phrase wound itself into his brain. Yeah, he did hate that. Dave would have known it too. He'd be standing with a wry grin on his face, thrilled to see somebody put one over on his too-serious partner.

Cody loved being right, maybe counted on it more than anything. Dave had always known it too, and loved when anybody could prove Cody wrong about something. Even when they did it gently, as Bree had this time, Dave got a kick out of it.

Cody had a feeling that somewhere his old partner was laughing. He shook his head and sighed, wondering if birthday cake and crow tasted good together.

Meanwhile he decided to enjoy the party. He hadn't intended to enjoy it, but nothing was turning out today the way he expected. Everything Bree had planned was going well. She stood in the middle of the fray, a bright sundress on and actually wearing a flower behind one ear. It looked exotic against her barely tanned skin and pale hair. Cody knew she hadn't put it there herself. Sarita had insisted that Bree needed a flower to match her own.

Bree... Cody's eyes tracked her down and studied her. She looked lovely. She was smiling and laughing and moving through the crowd. Everyone smiled back at her, talking to her as though she were an old friend. She knew just the right word to say to put someone at ease or make him or her happy. More than ever Cody wished for whatever magic she had. No, it wasn't magic. It was faith and happiness; two qualities that were in short supply in his life. Bree seemed to possess them both in abundance. Perhaps if he watched her long enough, he'd figure out how to get those things for himself.

She was talking to Ed and Charlotte now. Charlotte was making introductions, and Bree got a hug from Ed, who was as tall and thin as his wife was short and voluptuous. Cody could hear Ed asking Bree questions about why he hadn't seen much of her over at Island Community Church. Bree actually blushed as she answered.

"I want to hear this one myself." Cody came up to the group. "I expected you to be right in there with Shawn. You'd fit right in with the high school youth group."

"I probably would." Bree flashed him a brilliant smile. "Not that I appreciate your pointing it out, but I can't deny it. And there's no good reason that I haven't been there, Ed. Now that I've made your acquaintance I'll come Sunday, I promise."

"Great. We might even have a place for you in the praise band," Ed said. Bree's eyebrows furrowed. Clearly she was trying to figure out what Ed had meant. Even Cody was a little confused by this one.

"Praise band? I love them, but I don't play any instruments, and I only sing in the shower. Even then I make sure there's nobody else around to hear me murdering music."

Now Ed looked confused. "Charlotte said you

145

were a whiz at the keyboard. I was hoping to use you for backup."

"Wrong kind of keyboard, sweetheart." Charlotte laughed. "Computer, not musical."

"Rats. The two do go together a lot of times," Ed said. "Sorry I got mixed up."

"No problem." Bree patted Ed's hand. "I'm a lot more comfortable at the computer than I would be at anything else with a keyboard. I don't think I could manage 'Chopsticks' on a piano."

"If you're that good at the computer, maybe you could hang out with the high school group," Ed said. "They're always talking about starting a cybercafé in the high school room, or some other wild idea. More than once they've tried to talk me into a church Web site."

"That would be cool." Bree's eyes danced. "I'm trying to interest Cody in one, but I haven't gotten there yet."

"Not for lack of trying." Cody chuckled. "Which reminds me of something. I tried turning on the computer last night to do something and it started talking to me in martian or something. Did I mess anything up permanently?"

Bree's eyebrows shot up. "You turned it on by yourself? I'm impressed. I don't think you could have done any damage, permanent or otherwise. I might have had it set to access my online account. What did you do? Or what did it do?"

"Made strange noises, ending with hissing at me about the way I expect Gabe would've if I stepped on his tail."

"Modem," Ed and Bree chorused.

"He really is new to all this, if *I* can get ahead of him." Ed's smile was almost as bright as the sunshine bouncing off his balding head.

"Thanks, pal." Cody shot Ed a knowing wink. "You make me want to catch up. I mean, if *you* know about something before I do…"

"Hey, if somebody motivates you, I won't argue. You've definitely got me coming now, Ed. Just to thank you for getting Cody computer literate," Bree said.

"That would be something new," Charlotte said. "Think of how much we could do in the way of repeat customer information if we put it on the computer and Cody could actually use it with the rest of us."

"Charlotte, I get the idea." Cody waved her off. "Class will start tomorrow, okay?"

"Fine with me." Bree's smile was beautiful. Warm and genuine, soft lips curving in a way that made Cody want to touch them. But Bree was far too busy for anything like that. "Ready to help out with the piñata, Cody? We need somebody tall and quick to swing the rope."

"I think I can handle that," he said. "A lot better than I could the computer right now, anyway. Let's go bust some piñata." Following Bree back to the circle of the group was fun. The children surrounded her quickly, and almost all of them knew what to do with the piñata.

Cody was surprised at the number of children that were at the party. He knew that summer vacationers usually brought kids, but he wouldn't have guessed that a birthday party for a stranger would've been a draw for most of them to stay around the complex. Obviously he was wrong. Carlos was having the time of his life. As befitted his birthday-boy status he was blindfolded first, and Bree spun him around.

He wasn't peeking, but he was pretty good with a piñata bat. Carlos got in two good swings before Cody moved the bright papier-mâché donkey out of his way.

"Almost, Carlos." Bree clapped. "Now let's let somebody else have a try."

The next couple of kids, both vacationers, giggled a lot and didn't even scratch Mr. Donkey. "I do it." Sarita stepped up. "I gonna hit it hard."

She probably would, too, Cody decided. Bree didn't spin the little one around quite as much as she had some of the older kids. Sarita charged the piñata, curls bouncing out on both sides of the blindfold. Cody ducked out of the way of her first swing and directed the piñata into her path. The noise as the bat connected with the donkey's stuffed body was like that of a good line drive.

The donkey opened, pouring slips of paper, candy, little toys, and trinkets all over. Sarita dropped the bat and whipped off the blindfold the moment she heard her brother and the other kids shriek.

They were a good bunch of kids, Cody had to admit. Nobody was pushing anybody else out of the way, and most of the older ones even made sure Sarita had a good share of the loot for her success. Bree was laughing and shouting as much as the kids. Her flower drooped almost out of her hair and one strap of the sundress was askew as she helped the kids scramble for candy. It made a very appealing picture. Cody's fingers itched to right that strap and feel her warm skin against his fingers.

"I got a pencil," Cody heard one boy say.

"All right. A frog. It's green and orange." There were exclamations over the candy, and kids were taking slips of paper to their parents, who seemed happy over the free video rentals from a nearby store and the other goodies Bree had managed to convince local merchants to contribute.

"Who's ready for cake and ice cream?" Bree asked. She had straightened her dress and her hair and backed safely up against the picnic table before asking the thundering herd if they were ready to eat. Perhaps Bree was a lot more stable than he thought. Cody groaned inwardly. Maybe all his assumptions about Bree were off. He was going to have to tell her about Harry, he decided. When had he done this much confessing at one time?

"Not in recent memory," he muttered. But then never in recent memory had anybody like Bree blown into his life.

Bree sat staring at the computer screen carefully. Cody walked in and gave her a wry grin. "Didn't quite trust me on what I'd done to your baby, huh?" Cody folded his arms. He looked happier than usual.

Bree felt her mouth drop open. Cody was teasing her! No doubt about it. The twinkle in his eyes, the grin on his face...it was teasing pure and simple.

She regrouped quickly and shot him an answering smile. "There was a little bit of doubt, I admit it. But I was really more interested in how I'd left things set up to go online that easily. I didn't remember leaving things that way the last time I shut down, but apparently I did. So if there had been any damage due to your not knowing about something, it would have been as much my fault as yours."

"Gee, that's almost gracious." Cody's eyes still sparkled with laughter. "Does this mean we're on speaking terms again?"

"Sure. I can't stay mad at anybody long." Bree shrugged. "Even somebody who runs me through a police check."

The look on his face was priceless. His eyes widened, his jaw dropped open. He looked like a kid with his hand in the cookie jar. "Ouch. You found out about that. How?"

"Harry called. He thought he had Charlotte on this end, and before I could tell him otherwise, he was telling me that I didn't have a record. Which I already knew in the first place, by the way."

Cody looked so sheepish Bree could hardly keep from giggling.

"I expect you did." He groaned. "Is there any possible way you could see this from my end?"

"Hey, no problem. Checking out strange ladies you meet on dark roads makes sense even to me, Cody. You could have told me about it, though. I mean, I don't exactly look like an ax murderer, do I?"

Cody flashed her a wicked grin and waggled his eyebrows. "Ah, but Bree, darling, those are the folks you have to look out for. The ones that don't look like what they really are."

Darling? He'd called her *darling?* She felt her breathing go into double time…until the rest of his comment sank in: *"Those are the folks you have to look out for. The ones that don't look like what they really are."*

In that case we're both in trouble, Bree thought. Because like it or not, Cody was working his way into her heart deeper every day, even though he was still her gruff, snappish boss on the outside. What would he say if she told him that? Bree decided that particular revelation would have to wait until another day. Perhaps tomorrow...or far into the future. But like Scarlett O'Hara, Bree was completely content to give in to the idea that today was not the day to think about that particular problem.

No matter how much her conscience seemed to be disagreeing with her.

Ten

TWO DAYS AFTER THE BIRTHDAY PARTY BREE DECIDED SHE
wasn't meant for keeping secrets. It just wasn't in her
nature to be secretive and quiet. Talking all the time
and being open and friendly were much easier.

Even though she still felt that going online was
dangerous, Charlotte was so eager about learning
everything that Bree couldn't say no to her friend.
Surely something as simple as showing her how to sign
on with an Internet provider and get an account going
couldn't be dangerous, could it? Bree was back at the
keyboard before they'd both finished lunch even
though she knew that going online with her own
account could be risky. Charlotte's fantastic chocolate
cupcakes may have had something to do with it all, but
Bree refused to see them as a bribe. After eating one of

them and being promised the recipe, she couldn't refuse Charlotte.

Charlotte had plenty of valid points for learning everything. Her knowledge would help Island Breeze, as well as the church, so that she could take over when the secretary went on vacation. So Bree found herself showing Charlotte how to get on the Internet, cruise around to find things, and even how to write and send e-mail.

It all took quite a while on the computer, and Bree had no choice but to use her own online account to do everything Charlotte wanted to learn. After about twenty minutes Bree's palms felt sweaty. She could feel eyes boring into the back of her neck as if someone were watching her. *Get out of here now!* her common sense shrieked at her.

"This is really fun," Charlotte told her. "I can see how you could get way too involved in all this. I mean, look at it. You can do anything on the Net, can't you? I've seen places to order flowers, read books, listen to music, just about anything. What's that little doohickey blinking in the corner of the screen?"

Bree's heart pounded heavily. "It means I've got a message from somebody who's online right now. That person is letting me know he or she wants to chat."

"Sort of like a phone call without the phone? That's fascinating. How does it work?" Bree wanted to turn everything off and hide. But Charlotte meant so well. "I just click on the button," she said, doing just that. Relief made her nearly go limp when the instant message was from somebody at the community college in Indiana where she'd helped set up the computer lab. For a brief, scary moment she had been sure it would be Bo.

Hi, Bree. What's up? Scooter's message said. *Where did you wig out to?*

Someplace far away and very warm. I needed a break, Bree typed in. She was telling the truth without giving anything away. It felt good to talk to one of her buddies, especially somebody like Scooter. He was a shy young man she'd been encouraging in the Lord when she could. *You try Roy's church like I suggested?* she continued.

Too busy, Scooter shot back. *Big moneymaking hack job came my way. Looks like I can go to State after all.*

Way cool! Bree was sure it was time to sign off, even with her pal Scooter. *Stay in touch.*

"And that's how it works." She turned to Charlotte. "Scooter is about twelve hundred miles from here in Indiana. If I know him, he's probably sitting around in a nasty pair of ragged khaki shorts with a diet Mountain Dew, just looking for somebody to talk to. Aren't you glad this only transmits words and not pictures?"

Charlotte laughed. "Enchanted. Now what else can we do?"

"Something more practical. How about getting offline and starting to set up tickler lists that will tell us when to ask return customers if they want to book a week next year?"

Charlotte looked impressed. "We can do that?"

"That and a whole lot more." Bree got offline with relief. Usually her favorite place to be was on the computer, talking to somebody via the Internet. But right now every time she did it she felt like a sitting duck. The disconnect message on the screen when she signed off came as quite a relief.

"Closest airport?" Bo asked the travel agent on the other end of the line.

"Fort Myers, it looks like. You want to know how much to fly there from here?"

"Yeah. And available flights." The agent quoted him a price, and he winced. Finding Bree was getting expensive, between paying off Scooter and fronting the bill for his fancy equipment, and now going down to Florida and getting the elusive Ms. Trehearn.

Actually, he didn't need to get Bree herself. Not to bring her back to Indiana, anyway. "Yeah, book that," he told the agent. "And I'm going to need a rental car, too. How long? Make them both open-ended for now. I can't say how long I'm going to be down there." As long as it takes me to find her and those diskettes and do what I need to do.

"Thank you for using our services. Have a nice trip," the woman told him.

"Oh, I will. I definitely will." It would be even better once he was coming back. Once he could stop worrying about the mess Bree had made of his life and his business.

It was just too bad that Bree wouldn't be having a nice trip back as well.

"Anybody seen the change cup we keep out by the coffee urn?" Cody asked, coming into the office. The air-conditioning felt cool and welcome after being out on the pool deck. The answer to his question was obvious in the silence punctuated only by the clicking of computer keys.

Charlotte's red head and Bree's pale one bent over the computer told the story. Neither of them had been outside this morning. Charlotte's flying fingers on the keyboard showed too much enthusiasm.

"What? Outside?" she said, still looking at the screen. "Sorry, boss. You know me. I'll take any excuse to stay inside this time of year. And boy, has Bree ever given me the excuse."

Bree looked up and smiled at him. It was such a welcoming sight. Her bright blue eyes and sweet smile charmed Cody every time—and he was getting to the point where he just didn't bother fighting it anymore. It was too hard. It was almost like looking at Sarita when she wanted something. He knew that in the end he couldn't say no successfully to either of them.

"Could we maybe mount a tiny, small, trial publicity campaign for something?"

"Tiny and small, huh?" Cody put his hands on his hips. "Why do I get the feeling this is going to cost me money? And time?"

"It might." Bree's grin was wholly unrepentant. "But it will make you money too, and solve two problems at once. Charlotte has a great idea."

"So now it's Charlotte's idea, huh? Let me get something cold to drink and sit down with you two. I think I'm going to need the sustenance." Cody went back to the small refrigerator under the counter. With these two plotting and planning together there wouldn't be anything tiny and small about any idea they came up with. It would be more like gigantic and scary. He was going to need a very large, cold drink to handle this one.

"So, are these problems I'm aware of having already?" Cody sat down.

"One of them is," Bree said. "And the other one isn't. But you'll be happy to solve both of them, I'm sure."

"Start talking." He knew he sounded like he was

grilling a suspect back in the old days, but this scheme felt more like petty larceny than a brilliant idea at this point. He'd listen, but he wasn't sure how open he could be. *Help me listen with an open mind,* he thought, then almost dropped his drink. That thought felt suspiciously like prayer. And Cody was not a praying man anymore. The strangest part was that it felt good and right. Maybe this would be an okay idea after all." Okay, tell me. What are these two pressing problems?"

"Well, we've been going through all the files, and I've noticed something," Bree said. This sounded like a warm-up to Cody, and he wasn't disappointed. "You're never fully booked in July and August."

"That's true. Of course, with mosquitoes the size of B-52s and daily highs in the nineties, not to mention the beginning of hurricane season, it might just be that July and August are the least desirable times to visit the island," Cody said calmly.

"I can't argue with the bug part, but it doesn't really feel that much hotter to me then," Charlotte said. "And the few times we've gotten any real hurricane involvement, it's been a little later in the year."

"Okay, so explain the other problem." Cody took a sip of his drink. "I can tell they must counteract each other."

Bree wrinkled her brow. "I'm new at this marketing stuff. Motherboards are more in my line of work.

159

But how did you know that already?"

"Easy," Cody said. "You wouldn't bring up either problem unless you thought you had a solution. You do like fixing things. And so does Charlotte, although her favorite fixing-up projects involve people."

Charlotte made a face at him. "Now tell me one couple I've put together that hasn't been happy. I challenge you."

She had a point, but Cody wasn't about to tell her that. "The problem?"

"Charlotte came up with a way to fill those extra units in July and August. That is, if you're willing to cut the price just a little."

"How little?" Cody's eyes narrowed in suspicion. This had to cost him money. With these two involved together, there was just no other way around things.

"A hundred dollars a week?" Bree asked. "Would that be reasonable?"

"Maybe. How many do you think you could book?"

"Next year, probably all of them if we start now."

Cody choked on his drink. "All of them? This I want to hear."

"Christmas in July," the women chimed in together.

"See, Charlotte was telling me how hard it is for most pastors to get time off. They almost never do, and it's never at holidays, especially Christmas or Easter, because of the way things are set up."

"But most churches feel bad about that. I know the places we've been have said so. And they never know what to give the pastor for a gift at the end of the year, so it's usually money or a gift certificate or something. So when Bree asked what I thought we could do with those empty rentals in July and August, I just said..."

"Why not try to sell churches on the idea of giving their pastor a week's vacation on sunny Sanibel Island?" Bree grinned proudly, putting an arm around Charlotte. "And Charlotte has lists of congregations with e-mail addresses and home pages and everything. We could start advertising there first. I bet by Christmas we could fill every empty condo next summer."

It sounded goofy to Cody, but possible. "This isn't as strange as I expected. You two might actually have an idea here."

"See. What did I tell you?" Charlotte said. "Now what about taking Bree out to dinner to celebrate her brilliant idea?"

"It was half your idea," Bree said, sounding a little nervous.

"This wouldn't have anything to do with your other fixing-up ideas, would it, Charlotte?" Cody arched one eyebrow, glaring at her.

"Heavens, no," Charlotte said. "And I couldn't possibly go with you anyway. Ed has already offered to get Cuban sandwiches from the deli and bring a bunch of them over here so we can picnic with Marisa and the kids. He's trying to convince her that she could help out with vacation Bible school once she gets into a walking cast."

Cody groaned inwardly. So this *was* part of Charlotte's famous fix-ups. No sense in fighting; he'd just go quietly. "So when can I pick you up?"

Bree smiled shyly. Bree, shy? It was a new idea, but he liked it. "Six, maybe? I'm not much for fashionably late dinners. I get too hungry. Should I dress up?"

"Not too much. I thought we'd go off the tourist track as much as possible. Do you like conch?"

"Don't know. What is it?"

"You know those big shells you see people holding up to their ears to hear the ocean? Well, guys that look like giant sea snails live in there."

"And they're delicious," Charlotte said.

"I'll take your word for it." Bree grimaced. "I've never wanted to know too much about the animals I'm eating. One of these days I think I'm going to become a vegetarian because of that."

"Have it your way. And I'll see you at six." Cody got up and took his glass with him. All afternoon as he worked outside in the heat, deliciously distracting images tickled his brain. They came back every time he pictured the elusive Bree Trehearn dressed for dinner. It was going to be an interesting evening.

Cody cleaned up real nice. Bree was surprised at how he looked freshly showered, with a button-down shirt, and tailored shorts. Since they were sitting outside on what appeared to be an old boat dock, she could see that long pants would have been a hindrance.

Even in shorts Cody looked dressed up. His dark hair shone and he looked peaceful. Looking at him across the table at the restaurant, Bree decided this was the most relaxed she'd seen him in the time they'd known each other.

"We have to go out more often. You're actually smiling."

His forehead began to pucker. "Is it really that rare?"

"There's been a lot going on lately. And I guess I'm not the calmest companion," Bree said. "Are you usually more cheerful when I'm not around?"

Cody leaned back in his chair, looking deep in thought. "Cheerful? I guess not. Maybe more composed. I guess I wouldn't describe myself as a very cheerful person. Even when I was partnering with Dave, he was always telling me to lighten up."

"So he was the cheerful one of the two of you, hmm?" Bree was anxious to keep him talking about Dave in a good way.

"Almost always. Most cops get pretty jaded about the job and about people in general. Dave could still see the good in almost everybody, up until the day he died. Anybody, that is, who didn't pick on kids or animals."

"I think I would have liked to meet Dave." Bree leaned her elbows on the table and rested her chin on her hand. "Did he bring you down here?"

"Actually, he did. His family had vacationed here in the days before there was even a causeway...this was before his time, you understand...and just kept coming here. It's where he came when he wanted to unwind, and he got me doing it too."

"So how come you aren't unwound anymore?"

"Part of my ability to unwind died with Dave." Cody shrugged. "I find myself always on my guard. Something could happen, today, tonight, anytime. It's hard to relax knowing that."

Bree played with the straw in her iced tea. "Funny, I find that it's hard not to relax knowing that. I can't change what's going to happen. That's in God's hands. But I can enjoy what's here. For example, do those pelicans always hang out this close to shore?"

"Where there's trash floating in the water like this, some of them do. They know where to find food." Cody pointed out into the ocean. "And a lot of nights around sunset out here there are dolphins. We'll have to stick around for dessert and coffee so you can see them."

"I've never seen a dolphin, not for real." Bree was touched that he'd even think of it. "That's a television-only experience until today. Thanks, Cody."

"You're welcome. And I hope you like spicy food too, because I don't think I told you just how much red pepper the cook here puts in the conch chowder."

"I do like it, most of the time. But I might want another glass of iced tea for a backup." Bree hoped her nose didn't turn red while she was eating. It was so unattractive. Nobody ever wants to kiss somebody with a red nose.

The iced tea she was drinking nearly went down sideways along with an ice cube. Bree choked. *Kiss somebody?* Like, kiss Cody? Where had that come from? She had to slow down here. They'd gone from dessert and coffee to kissing in her mind in a nanosecond. "And we haven't even seen those dolphins yet," she muttered. It promised to be a very interesting evening. She only hoped she was up to it.

Eleven

BREE WAS STILL GETTING USED TO SANIBEL ISLAND. IT WAS part Florida tourist haven, part small-town America, and she was never sure where one ended and the other began, but with each trip through town she got more used to the combination.

She wondered how people like Ed and Charlotte handled the diversity. It had to be hard to pastor a church where a third of the congregation wouldn't be there the next week, or maybe ever again. Still, she thought as she watched Ed greet people before services at Island Community Church, it didn't seem to bother him much. He was open and warm with everyone.

The congregation might change weekly, but Ed's church was a friendly place to be. And Bree was starting to feel almost at home there. She also was getting used to Florida architecture, which planned for hurricanes by making things more sprawling than sweeping upwards. Island Community Church was a perfect example of that: spread out in a comfortable complex of buildings that seemed to have something for everyone. Shawn took pride in showing her the youth room where he hoped to lure Bree after services and get her to talk about starting a cybercafé there. Carlos and Ana, who had tagged along to church, were more interested in playing games on the computer than talking technical things, or even heading in to services.

Once they got into the church itself, however, Carlos and Ana were happy to be there. The praise band was playing before services, and folks greeted friends and welcomed strangers. Shawn made sure that several people got introduced to Bree, and they were all very nice to her.

It was the first time in her life Bree could remember feeling shy. Some little voice in the back of her head kept urging her not to be so friendly or outgoing. It kept reminding her that she needed to keep a low profile and stay quiet. Still, this was the Lord's house— surely she was safe here, of all places? So she loosened up a little and gave way to the enjoyment of other people's company.

It was a nice place to be, and Ed had plenty of help making folks feel welcome whether they were there for a day or a lifetime. Ana loved the music. Carlos controlled most of his wiggling, and Bree felt right at home. She'd been away from church much too long, she decided as she stood with the crowd in line to greet Ed at the door.

"Well, we got you here after all. Good job, Shawn." Ed pumped her hand and patted Shawn on the back at the same time. He bent down to talk to the kids, who gave him a progress report on their mom.

Ed assured them that he'd stop by soon to see her, and that once she was in a real walking cast they would have to find a way to get her to come with them. "We will," Ana promised him, looking up with a smile that made Bree's heart glad. "She'll like the music, and so will Sarita."

"And we get pancakes. Bree is taking us," Carlos said with a shy smile.

"I bet you can eat a lot of pancakes." Ed ruffled his hair. "You be good now, okay?"

"Sure," Carlos said. Ana nodded but managed to convey without saying anything what she thought her brother's chances of being good in public really were.

Carlos proved her wrong several times in the next hour. First he was a good kid in the youth room, where the teenaged girls cooed over him while Shawn got Bree interested in the intricacies of the computer system. She didn't spend long there because she didn't want Carlos and Ana munching cookies with the teenagers instead of eating something more nutritious in the restaurant.

Even when they had to wait a little while for a table at Sanibel Café, which was popular with folks after services, Carlos was the perfect gentleman. Or at least as perfect as anybody just barely six could be expected to be. "This is nice," he said, finally ensconced in a booth next to Shawn. "Can we bring Mama back next week when she gets that other cast on?"

"If she does, I think we can." Bree glanced at the menu. "Would you like chocolate milk with your pancakes?"

"Sure." Carlos's face beamed. It seemed to be his all-purpose phrase. "Mama said no soda, but she didn't say no chocolate milk."

"Then we'll have a round for everybody," Bree told the young waitress, who seemed to be flirting a little with Shawn. "That is, unless Shawn wants coffee."

"No, I guess I'll have chocolate milk with the rest of you. Strong bones and all." Shawn flashed their waitress a grin. "Besides, I need to set a good example for the kids, right, Bree?"

"Right." She acted as if that was the only reason he was turning down coffee. She'd never seen him drink it at home but thought it would boost his mature image if the young girl, who was probably his high school classmate, saw him turn it down. The waitress took their orders and came back with four foamy glasses in a short time. Shawn was the first to need a refill.

"Now we need a walk," Bree told everybody when they left the café. "That much pancakes and sausage and bacon demands some exercise."

It was fun window-shopping on Sunday afternoon in the little plazas down Periwinkle. People on bikes, on foot, and on Rollerblades milled around with the shoppers. One plaza was filled with huge wrought-iron cages where bright parrots and macaws talked to folks passing by. It put a decidedly tropical spin on Sunday afternoon.

After seeing notices in three different windows, Bree turned to Shawn. He was helping Carlos untie a knotted shoelace. "So tell me about the Fourth of July here. What do people do?"

Shawn shrugged. "Same as everyplace, I guess. There are fireworks at night on a boat, way out from the beach. None are allowed on the island except sparklers and kids' stuff. Too dry and too dangerous for the other things. And of course the parade."

"Parade? As in marching bands and everything?" Bree felt about Ana's age. "I've never been in a Fourth of July parade."

Shawn laughed. "Me neither. What makes you think you're going to be in one now?"

171

"Don't the local businesses have floats? I mean, Island Breeze Condos has to have something in the parade, doesn't it?"

Shawn shook his head. "We never have before. Dad doesn't see the point in goofy stuff like that. He usually helps with crowd control that day; the police need every trained person they can get."

"Sounds like a real blast," Bree said, aware she was grumbling. "Think I could change his mind on the float thing?"

Shawn shrugged. "With anybody else, I'd say no. But hey, I never saw a birthday party at Island Breeze until last week, either. None that the guests got invited to, anyway. If you think you can pull off something this big, go for it. Just don't get me involved until Dad stops arguing."

Certifiable. It was the only word Cody could come up with to describe Bree's latest scheme. She looked adorable telling him about it. Those blue eyes looked even wider than Gabe's. He could tell because she had the furry fuzzball on her lap while she described in detail why Island Breeze should have a float in the Fourth of July parade.

The cat, in his inimitable way, seemed to agree with all this. At least he let Bree bounce him around in her lap while she gestured and explained. "Think of all the great free advertising. And Shawn tells me that the kids love the parade because all the floats throw candy and stuff. He and Ana could walk alongside handing out flyers if we put one together. And Marisa could ride in the back and wave."

Cody felt more confused than he usually did around Bree. It probably had something to do with the fact that he couldn't help watching her appealing mouth move, instead of listening to the words that came out of it. "Back of what? I missed what you wanted to use for this float. Not the pickup truck, that's for sure. And nobody on the island has a convertible except the mayor and the guy who owns that big restaurant up on the point near Captiva, and I expect both of them are using theirs."

"You just *look* grumpy." The pout on Bree's face was a mirror image of Gabe's face after he'd just woken up from a nap. "You don't really feel that grouchy, do you?"

"Of course I do. And I repeat my question. What on earth do you intend to ride in this parade, Bree?"

She looked at him as if he had no imagination at all. Of course, according to Bree he didn't have any, so it was an easy look for her to give him. "I'm sure I've said it at least three times. Mel said we could use his big red pedal surrey. Free, if I worked on his office computer just a little bit. It's got a sticky CD-ROM drive."

"Is that easy to fix? I don't want you trading much time for a pedal surrey for a couple of hours."

"More like a couple of days." Bree shook her head. Why did she have to look so enchanting when she did that? Maybe if she wasn't so appealing Cody could tell her no more often. "We have to decorate the pedal surrey. Can't ride the whole parade with a plain one, can we?"

"Oh, *surely* not." It was so easy to tease her. "The crowd on the reviewing stand would boo."

She looked almost shocked. "Would they really? Are they that picky here?"

Cody laughed. Not only was it easy to tease her, it was fun, too. "Not really. But admit it, I had you going there for a minute, didn't I?"

Bree's shoulders drooped, and her mobile lips shaped into a definite pout. "You did. And I didn't even realize it. Maybe you're right. Maybe I ought to just tell the kids they can't ride in a parade."

Were there tears in her eyes? Suddenly Cody felt like a total heel. "You told the kids already?"

"Of course. You should have seen Sarita. She was so happy. And now I have to tell her we can't do the parade now. She'll be crushed, Cody. That sweet little face looking up at you. I'm going to tell her that Mr. Cody is the bad man who won't let her ride in his parade."

Cody felt about two inches tall. If there was anything that made him feel worse than disappointing Bree, it was disappointing Sarita. "Well, maybe it isn't such a silly idea after all. Maybe we could swing a few bucks for some decorations and a couple of sacks of safety suckers from the outlet mall."

Bree grinned. "You mean it?"

Cody shrugged. "Go ahead. I hate to disappoint my darling Sarita." It was almost as painful as disappointing Bree...

"And you won't." Gabe jumped off her lap as she bounded up and swept over to hug him. "She'll be so happy to hear about it once I tell her."

Even though Bree's embrace felt marvelous, Cody pulled away slightly. Her warm, soft hands slipped away from his neck. "What do you mean, once you tell her? I thought you were already planning to make me the evil demon of this little piece of melodrama."

Bree dropped a kiss on his forehead. "You're not the only one who can tease around here, mister. I may have taken my major in practical stuff like computers and business at school, but I took drama for fun."

That was it. Cody wouldn't be tricked this many times in one day. He sat down and pulled Bree down onto his lap. She shrieked in laughter and landed on top of him with a satisfying thump. It would have been a great move if he hadn't been in an office chair with wheels. The chair threatened to dump both of them as Bree struggled to get her balance.

She smelled so good. A little bit of sea breeze mixed with a delicate floral perfume. The scent was as elusive as the woman herself. Cody slid one hand around the back of her neck, gently pulling her down to meet him. "Come here." The husky rasp of his voice surprised him.

Bree obeyed him without argument. Wide eyes fringed with impossibly long, dark lashes swam into focus directly in front of his face. "I'm here," she said softly. "What do you want, Cody?"

"More than I can have. More than I'll take." He ached to say so much more, but it just wasn't time. Her lips were soft as petals when he kissed her. And like the delicate rose Bree reminded him of, he didn't want to crush her. But she felt so right in his arms. It was a long moment before Cody could master himself and pull away from her a little. He met her gaze, taking in the dreamy look in her eyes. She was so amazing…so trusting… "Should I apologize for that?"

Bree looked bemused. One finger strayed to the sweet lips he had so recently kissed. "Probably. But only if I can apologize too. Because it takes two people to kiss like that, Cody. We can't possibly do it again, but once was quite an experience. Thank you."

"For the kiss or the parade?"

"For both," she said softly, moving to stand, careful not to upset the precarious chair. She turned to walk away, flashing a smile that made his toes curl. "Definitely for both."

"Are we really going to ride this in a parade?" Ana looked up at Bree.

She wore the biggest smile Bree had seen on her so far. Bree looked at it, long and hard, so that she could tell Cody all about it in detail in case it didn't last. She knew that he wanted to see the little girl happy.

"Yes, Ana, we are really going to ride this in a parade. Mr. North said so. And you know everything that he says really works out." Cody was that kind of man, and Bree and Ana both recognized it.

Ana smiled even wider, looking up at the red-and-white-fringed top of the pedal surrey. "This is going to be so much fun. Do we get to decorate it too?"

"We sure do. But we have to be creative with that. We can't spend a lot of money, and it has to look nice."

Ana waved a small hand dismissively. "Then we'll get Mama to help. She can make something out of nothing any day. When Carlos and Sarita were babies they always had tons of toys, and we never had any money. Mama can decorate this thing easy."

She probably could, Bree decided. And Ana was

right. This was going to be so much fun. It would be more fun once they finished getting the pedal surrey the three more blocks to Island Breeze. It was probably three-quarters of a mile from Mel's to the condo complex, and Bree's legs were getting tired from pedaling. She could just imagine how Ana felt.

It wasn't as difficult as pedaling a bicycle uphill, but it was different. The pedal surrey looked like a golf cart with no motor, only lighter and airier. There were no sides, and the slatted seats were designed for light weight as much as comfort. "Next time can I steer?" Ana asked from her place at the front passenger seat.

"I don't know about that. I'm still getting the hang of it myself," Bree told her. "I don't know what Mel would say if I turned over the wheel to somebody who wasn't even in fifth grade yet."

"Rats." Ana looked out her side of the surrey and ran her fingers up the red tubular metal frame. "Do you think it has a name?"

"What, this surrey? I have no idea. What would you name it, if it were yours?"

Ana smiled again and looked up at the swaying fringe. "I'm not sure. Something with *bella* at the end."

"Hmm. Beautiful. That would fit. It is beautiful, isn't it? What about Anabella?"

Ana's face wrinkled up. "No way. I'm not beautiful, Bree. This surrey may be, but I'm not."

Bree reached over and ran a finger down her short nose. "Of course you are. Everybody is beautiful, Ana. You just have to know how to look. Jesus loved you enough to die for you. How can you be anything but beautiful?"

Ana smiled again, shyly this time. "I see what you mean. You don't mean movie-star beautiful. You mean heart beautiful. Mama says you're beautiful on the outside, but it's even better because you're beautiful on the inside. That's heart beautiful, isn't it?"

"Right." Bree swallowed past a lump in her throat. "That's heart beautiful. And it's very nice of your mother to say so." *Now I only have to live up to her expectations and Ana's.* It wasn't going to be easy.

One more block of pedaling. Bree wasn't sure she could live up to being "heart beautiful" for Ana and Marisa all the time, but she knew she could pedal the surrey. So she looked ahead and kept pedaling while Ana began to whistle.

The Fort Myers airport was pretty small. It wasn't like the big international terminals Bo was used to. There were a few gates, a few luggage returns, and a couple of places to buy expensive coffee and T-shirts with flamingo heads on them. Then you were out in the hot sunshine, surrounded by palm trees. Quite a difference from Indiana.

He stood watching the luggage carousel go around again. For a small airport, you'd think they would be more efficient. It had been twenty minutes at least since his flight had landed, and there was still no sign of his bag.

Bo's strategic position in front of the spot where the bags slid onto the carousel wasn't an accident. The contents of that bag were too important to risk some eager teenager grabbing it, mistaking it for his shorts and sandals. If anybody found the semiautomatic deep in one compartment he was in a world of trouble. Fortunately he looked like such an upright citizen that he didn't attract any attention. So far, so good.

Finally the hunter green bag tipped over the side of the chute and slid down. It made it about four feet around the carousel, then Bo picked it up, righted it on the floor, and got it rolling behind him on the tiled airport floor.

He took the suitcase over to the pay phones where one phone miraculously had its yellow pages still intact. Bo paged through the book, looking casual. Most observers probably would think he was looking for rental cars. Probably not too many tourists checked computer repair shops first, rental cars second. But then most tourists weren't looking for somebody like Bree Trehearn. Bo was not only looking, but he was going to find her, quickly. He started humming tunelessly as he ripped the two pages quietly out of the directory. It was a start.

Twelve

"DO YOU LIKE THE FLOWERS?" ANA ASKED, NEARLY DANCING beside Cody. "We made them out of bags."

"Out of bags? They look too pretty to be made out of bags." Cody had to go touch one. The surrey was decorated with garlands of flowers, obviously artificial but pretty, in red and yellow. Green plastic of some kind formed vines and branches that draped the flowers over the top and sides of the surrey.

A large sign on each side said Island Breeze Vacations in bold letters. Ana and her little sister seemed to be as decorated as the surrey. Cody wondered where Bree had gotten the paper leis the girls wore. For that matter he'd wondered briefly where she'd gotten half the stuff, but he hadn't paid that much attention. Bree had told him that she would take care of getting what they needed one way or another. For a woman like Bree, whose faith and integrity meant everything to her, Cody knew that was as good as cash and a contract for most people. Besides, whenever he had an odd moment to daydream, he was still replaying that wonderful kiss they'd shared. That was a much better image to focus on than wondering where she got the things to decorate a pedal surrey.

Wherever Bree had gotten all the odds and ends that she and Marisa and the kids had transformed into beautiful decorations, it had kept her busy. Cody hadn't seen her without something in her hands—or muttering to herself over some part of the decorations—for most of a week. Even her beloved computer needed dusting at the end of that time. Bree put all her energy into decorating the surrey and getting the kids to practice riding in it. That and getting them all outfits that matched the colors in the decorations.

Carlos drew the line at being dressed all in red and yellow like the girls. He conceded to a red and yellow striped shirt, as long as it had some navy blue in it to go with his denim shorts. And Cody knew for a fact that Shawn wasn't going to be color coordinated, unless you counted his red T-shirt.

The four girls were a picture, though. Ana and Sarita had bright printed sundresses in red, yellow, and white, and red sandals to match. Bree and Marisa both had tops of the same print as the girls' sundresses and big straw hats with garlands of flowers around the brims. Marisa had a bright red skirt that went close to the ground to disguise her cast, while Bree had red shorts since she was one of the pedal team. Cody had to admit she looked downright delectable in those red shorts.

Bree crossed her arms and grinned up at Cody. "Shawn and I will do most of the actual work. Of course, Carlos is helping whenever one of us needs a break."

"Of course." No matter how sturdy Carlos was, he was going to have a hard time filling in for Shawn or Bree. Still, if it made him feel good to be a member of the team, Cody wasn't going to be the one to burst his bubble. And he was a strong little kid; he probably could pedal for several blocks with an adult helping.

Cody shook his head. His attitude had changed so much since Bree came into his life. Optimism came with little practice these days. His once cynical nature seemed to take a break now and then, no longer coloring the way he looked at every event. Best of all, he was talking to God again. They weren't on the close speaking terms they'd been on when he was partnering with Dave, but Cody had to admit that God felt much closer now than he had in years.

Yeah, well, who moved? He could hear a wry voice in

183

his head that sounded a lot like Dave. It was easy to answer that question. Cody had put up the wall in the first place, and now just maybe he was taking it down, brick by brick.

Bree had so much to do with that wall destruction. He wondered if it would've gotten done at all without her. Not at this speed, that's for sure. He had to tell her about this. That would be harder than telling her the other part of what he needed, or at least wanted, to tell her. Cody needed to tell Bree soon how he felt about her. Seeing that he wasn't the most expressive guy in the world, chances were good Bree had no idea how he felt.

It wasn't until he saw this crazy pedal surrey all decorated, with the kids dancing around it and Bree and Marisa sitting inside fastening on the last of the flowers, that Cody realized how he felt. How could he not love someone who had made these kinds of changes in his life? And how could he not tell her? *Tomorrow after the parade. I'll tell her then.*

He could picture the moment. They'd finish the parade route and Bree would be flushed from the pedaling and waving. She'd be laughing and that wide-brimmed hat would be askew. Long silver-gold strands of her hair floating on the breeze, eyes sparkling. It would be perfect.

Cody smiled. For the first time in his years on

Sanibel Island he was looking forward to a holiday parade. Even doing crowd control tomorrow didn't sound so bad anymore. He wondered how late Island Blooms was open this evening. Maybe he could even get a nice bouquet and tuck it in the refrigerator to wait for tomorrow. It was the only way flowers would last in this heat.

No, that wouldn't do. Having him go so far out of character as to buy flowers would just startle Bree. He wanted to make her laugh, make her smile, have her throw those supple arms around his neck. He didn't want to startle her. At least not at first. No, this particular feat would require some serious plotting and planning.

Cody smiled the rest of the afternoon.

Bo was getting frustrated. It was a new feeling. Nobody frustrated him this much. Of course it had to be Bree doing it; the only times in recent memory he'd felt this frustrated, it had been because of her. Florida was too hot to mess around in. Too hot, and this part of it had bugs the size of poodles. There were plenty of reasons why Bo had never considered Florida a place to visit.

Everybody was so friendly. They wanted to know all of your business, too. It made his skin crawl. Bo felt like hiding out someplace dark and cloudy for a few days where nobody would ask him any questions. Once he got his hands on Bree he was going to do just that. Now if he could just verify that she was really where he thought she was, things would be all right.

She had proven tricky to find. Once Scooter had narrowed things down to this part of the world, Bo was pretty sure that when he found her it would be in Fort Myers near a shopping mall and some main drag. There weren't enough places to buy hardware or make a living anyplace else.

And it wasn't like Bree could hide out for long on whatever money she had saved. At least not the Bree he knew. The little fool never had more than pocket change. She was always giving things away and fixing things for free because of her warped values.

If Bo had thought more about those values, he'd never have trusted her with a major overhaul of his hard drive. Bree might be the queen of the space cadets, but she'd found some way around his safeguards and passwords into his files. Not only that, but once she'd uncovered them, she had also been able to decipher them. She must have. It was the only reason for what had happened. . .for them all self-destructing the first time he pulled them up after getting the hard drive back from Bree.

For a few short moments after his temper tantrum that day, Bo had started packing to leave town. If Bree had deciphered those files, odds were good she'd gone to the cops. It sounded like a good idea maybe to go to Idaho and hang out for a while until things cooled down. Then it hit him. Bree was the all-time goody-goody, but she also was the first to give a guy second and third chances, whether he deserved them or not. After all, they were friends. Little Miss Goodness and Light wouldn't turn a friend in to the cops. Oh, no. She'd just do something like make his files self-destruct as a way to give him time to see the error of his ways. Anybody else would have planned it as a distraction, but not Bree. She was just too nice to turn in a friend to the police, even if he was breaking the law big time.

Bo snorted. That was a shame for her. Because Bo wasn't too nice to do what he needed to do. He wasn't nice at all. And after two days of looking for Bree Trehearn, he'd found her in the most unlikely place. Now all he had to do was figure out a way to get to her. That would be the hard part, but not too hard. No job would be too hard if it meant he got his files back and got a little revenge on Bree.

Doing both at the same time would be very, very rewarding.

The island was working its magic on Bree again. Today it was only one part tropical paradise and about three parts small-town America. No small town she'd ever been in before had this much hoopla on the Fourth of July.

Independence Day had always struck her as a great reason to have a holiday. Where else but America could you celebrate this many freedoms at once? She gave thanks to God that she could celebrate so many of them.

It was fun to put the last touches on the pedal surrey with the Montoya family, with Charlotte and Shawn helping. Bree turned to Charlotte. "Sure I can't talk you into going with us?"

"No, I really have to ride on the church float," Charlotte said. "Besides, my pink would clash with your red and yellow."

"Maybe." Shawn whooped from the other side of the surrey. "But not as much as my black and purple will."

"You wouldn't dare. Would you?" If anyone else had made the threat, even Cody, Bree would've known they wouldn't ruin a carefully crafted color scheme that way. But with Shawn, all things were possible. His own natural daring and Cody's parenthood made him an interesting fellow.

His grin was Shawn's answer. "No, I wouldn't. But the look on your face was worth more than doing it anyway. Do you know you panic just about the same way Gabe does?"

Bree pushed a breath out forcefully. "Huh. Now when have you seen him panic?"

"When I had to rescue him yesterday from the bathroom. Do you know that goofy cat can get up on the top of the shower doors? Only problem is, he can't get down. There are some distances a feline can jump up but they won't go back where they came from."

"I know. And I thought I'd cured him of that. Thanks, Shawn."

"Anytime," Shawn said affably, going back to his last-minute polishing. "Let me change that—almost anytime. I am not nearly as much of a morning person as my dad. Anytime after eight in the morning. Why are you laughing, Bree?"

"At the thought of your dad being called a morning person. That first morning I came over for breakfast I would have thought for certain I'd woken up Dracula."

Shawn laughed. "That was when he didn't know you at all. Knowing Dad, he probably thought we were being invaded. You're lucky he didn't come into the kitchen with a gun drawn."

Bree stiffened. "Would he do that?"

"If he thought somebody he cared about was in danger he would. Not just for fun. He won't even let me target shoot until after I'm eighteen. And he keeps all the ammunition locked in one safe, the gun in another. He's cautious."

"I'm glad. Where guns are concerned, cautious is good." Bree shivered a little, even in the Florida heat, remembering Bo's passion for guns. He loved them and treated them with disrespect, and it had always struck her as a very poor combination.

"You can't be cold," Marisa said. "It is so hot out here you could fry things on the street."

"*Eggs,* Mama. That's what people say here. That you can fry *eggs* on the *sidewalk*."

Bree marveled at the changes in Ana during the last two weeks. She was getting her childhood back. Ana smiled and bubbled. She loved having new clothes, and like all the rest of the female crew members today, she had her nails, both fingers and toes, polished a bright red to go along with the decorations. Even Sarita had red toenails peeking out from her sandals, a fact that made her giggle once in a while. And when Sarita stopped and giggled today, Ana did too. She was a far cry from the dreadfully serious little girl Bree had met in June.

"That's right, Ana. It is hot enough to fry eggs on the sidewalk. Not that we're going to try it or anything. So that isn't why I'm shivering." Bree turned to Marisa.

"My grandma would have said a goose walked over your grave," Charlotte broke in. Explaining that phrase to Marisa and the giggles that ensued relieved Bree of any need to explain why she was shivering. For once she was glad to have an outgoing friend like Charlotte whose outlandish comments could come at the most opportune moments.

By the time the parade was ready to start, Bree was glad to have a friend like Cody, too. It was his pickup truck that took the pedal surrey to the parking lot where they would join the parade. After helping Shawn wrestle the ungainly thing down from the bed of the truck, he turned to Bree.

"Anything else you need me to do today? Hand-to-hand combat with an alligator? Draining a couple of swamps?"

"Oh, it wasn't that hard," she scoffed. "And we all appreciate it so much. Don't we, girls?"

Everyone mobbed the sweating Cody at once. He got hugs and kisses from all the women from Sarita on up to Charlotte. "Okay, so you all appreciate me." He chuckled. He had somehow managed to hold on to Bree for just a moment after everyone else had mobbed him. The nearness of him, even sweaty and hot like this, made Bree's pulse quicken.

Those golden brown eyes searched hers. "You'll be careful steering this thing, won't you? And you'll stay right on the parade route and not try to pop wheelies or anything?"

Bree giggled. "This vehicle couldn't pop a wheelie anywhere, anytime. You don't have to worry about that part."

Cody gave her a quick squeeze before letting go. "Good. Something has me a little uptight today. I don't know what it is, but I'm a little concerned about you. Anything you want to share with me?"

"Nothing," Bree said, aware of the speed of her reply. "I'll try to be good. And careful," she promised. "You do the same, okay? Directing traffic during a parade sounds more dangerous than being in it."

Cody shrugged. "So this trust you're always talking about is one way, hmm? Thanks, Bree."

It pained Bree to see his expression, but this was the only way she knew how to protect him, the Montoyas, and Island Breeze. "I trust you, Cody. After the parade, we'll talk. And you will be careful, right?"

Cody's expression was enigmatic. "I've done it so many times I could probably do it in my sleep. The little kids on bikes are the worst part. Wave at me when you come by, okay?"

"Sure," Bree told him. "Stay cool and I'll see you in a couple hours." She reached up on tiptoe and kissed him quickly on the nose. "Oops. Red lipstick." She wiped it until there weren't any smudges.

"Thanks. Be good." His concern made her almost as shivery as thinking of Bo had earlier. For a moment she almost told Cody everything she was worried about. But there wasn't time now. Sarita tugged on her mother's dress, needing a cold drink before they got started. Carlos and Shawn chased each other around the surrey, and Ana stood with her hands on her hips, indignant with them both. It was time to get this show on the road.

For the first time, Cody was having fun directing traffic during a parade. The sights and sounds were new to him because he was seeing them the way Bree and the Montoya clan would see them.

Music from the larger floats sounded cheerful. Charlotte and Ed waved when the flatbed pulling the praise band from Island Community Church came through. Cody even waved back.

Okay, so it was hot and buggy. That was to be expected of Sanibel in July. But why had he never noticed before how much all the little kids enjoyed this parade? Did everybody throw hard candy and things like that? The kids scrambled for treats. One little boy about four had filled his baseball cap and now was working on his shorts pockets. This was really fun.

About a block away he could finally see Bree and the pedal surrey. She was having as good a time as the kid with the full baseball cap was. Cody reached up and waved, and she waved back. She was so beautiful. Her full smile lit up the area around her.

Bree turned to Shawn, who was sitting on the other half of the front seat and pedaling slowly. He looked through the crowd and waved with her. Cody

wondered if anybody else could have gotten his intro-
verted teenager to be in a parade like this. Probably
not. Bree was one of a kind. She reached into a bag that
Marisa held out behind the front seat and got a handful
of candy. With a throw worthy of a softball star she
tossed the goodies out to the kids, who scrambled for
it, shrieking with laughter. While they were still working on picking it all up, Bree dug in and got another
handful. This time she tossed it harder than the first
batch, so it landed right in front of the two smaller kids
who couldn't get into the fray quite as deep. That was
Bree, all right.

Cody watched all the kids pick up candy. He could
hear Bree laughing with them. When he turned around
again to look at her, he started to call out—but her
expression stopped him.

For a moment Cody thought maybe Bree was getting heatstroke. She'd gone still and pale, one hand
frozen in a wave. It was all Cody could do to keep from
leaping into the parade and charging down the half
block to see what was wrong.

In a moment Bree turned to Shawn. She said
something briefly to him, and he nodded. Then she did
something that was odd even for Bree. She climbed out
of the surrey and took off. One moment she was driving, the next she had pushed through the crowd on
Cody's side of the street, about half a block down the

road. The crowd on Periwinkle swallowed her up and she was gone.

Cody looked across the street to see if something she had seen had startled her. There wasn't anything unusual there. Just more parade watchers, including one heavyset man in his late twenties. If anybody seemed out of place in the parade crowd, it was this guy. He wore a dark plaid sport shirt and dark pants, and his face was flushed but not tanned. And he seemed to be glaring at the spot where Bree disappeared.

That was all the encouragement Cody needed. He blew his whistle and started across the street in front of the group of Boy Scouts with their banner. It took a moment to untangle himself from the leaders of the group as they stopped and started, trying to avoid him.

By the time he got to the other side of the street, the man was gone. No one seemed to know who he was. "He didn't say anything the whole time. Didn't dive for candy either," a small boy near the lamppost told Cody. For the kid, the fact that the man hadn't gone after the candy seemed to be the most amazing part.

Cody looked at the parade, starting to move again. There was no sign of Bree anywhere. Shawn had moved to the driver's seat of the pedal surrey, with Carlos next to him. "Did she tell you anything before she took off?" Cody asked Shawn.

Shawn shrugged. "Nothing. She just got real quiet and pale. Then she told me to take over and she split. Do you know what's going on, Dad?"

"Not a clue. Finish this last block and a half of the parade, and wait for me in the parking lot there, okay? I'm going to try and find her."

"Okay. This is weird," Shawn said. "I'll take care of everybody else."

Cody was sure he would do just that.

Now all he had to do was find Bree.

Thirteen

CODY WAS STARTING TO PANIC, SOMETHING HE ALMOST never did. He'd been looking for Bree for over twenty minutes and there was still no sign of her. How did a woman on foot vanish so completely? The sun hat and red shorts should be easy to find even in a crowd, but there was no sign of Bree anywhere.

The crowds thinned to almost nothing as he walked away from Periwinkle. He wished the island had issued him one of those dumb golf carts that some of the crowd control guys and parade handlers rode. Then he'd at least be a little faster than Bree.

Where could she be? Cody looked up and down each intersection with a practiced sweep of the area. Still no Bree. After four blocks he was getting closer and closer to the western edge of the island. In about three more he'd hit beach, and he still hadn't found her.

Could the guy who scared her, whoever he was, have an accomplice? Cody's neck prickled at the thought of somebody grabbing Bree and taking her off the island. He knew it couldn't be the man they both saw at the parade, because there was almost no way to get across the street for the two-mile length of the parade. One person could do it on foot, but no vehicles were going across the island right now unless they were police or fire. So if Bree had been snatched by somebody, it had to be another person besides the suspicious man Cody remembered from the parade.

Whoever that man was, Cody already didn't like him. The man had the look of someone up to no good. Cody stopped on the asphalt path alongside the street. No bikes or Rollerbladers had moved him off so far. In two blocks he'd reach the sand.

Being that close to the beach gave Cody an inspiration. Suddenly he knew where to go. He cut down a side street and walked as quickly as he could without getting light-headed in the heat. Two blocks over, one down, and he was at that spot of road where he'd found Bree the first time he met her.

The entrance to the public beach was less than a block ahead. There, outside a concrete shelter where they had both gotten soaked the night of her arrival on Sanibel, sat Bree Trehearn.

Her hat was in the sand at her feet and her hair was mussed. There were sweaty smudges on her face...from wiping away tears? She was oblivious to the families streaming away from the parade and moving on to a day at the beach now that the parade was almost over.

Cody came up next to her and sat down. "Tell me all about it. Everything. There has to be a reason for bolting like that, lady. I want to hear it. Now."

Bree drew in a ragged breath. "Okay. But this may take a while. It's kind of a long, complicated story. And you're not going to understand some of it no matter how I tell it, so just take it on faith, okay?" Her blue eyes pleaded with him.

"I'll take it on faith for long enough to hear your story, Bree. Then I may ask a lot of hard questions." Cody crossed his arms. "Start talking."

Bree hardly knew where to start. Cody looked so angry. "When you were a policeman, did you ever have to deal with hate groups?"

Bree could tell from his puzzled look that he already wanted to ask what this had to do with anything. "Like what? The Klan, white supremacists, that kind of stuff? Not in Tampa. Not anybody who meant business, anyway."

"Well, they still have roots in Indiana." It had been

painful for her to admit that. To find out about such a group and its inner workings while repairing a friend's computer came as even more of a shock. "I never thought about Bo being into anything illegal—"

Cody stopped her. "Bo?"

She nodded. "A customer, and a friend. Or at least I thought he was. He was a little odd and pretty quiet at times, but he seemed to be searching for something. I tried to make him see that Jesus was the answer to that empty spot in his heart." She drew in a ragged sigh. "He was so lonely." She shook her head. "No, let me correct that. Bo was always alone. He didn't seem all that lonely, more like a very self-sufficient type."

"Classic sociopath," Cody muttered. "Anybody could have seen that. Anybody who didn't trust the entire world. Still, I bet it drove you crazy."

Bree was surprised that Cody hadn't exploded into anger yet. He was trying very hard to be understanding, and she could see what it cost him. Seeing his controlled fury made her feel worse than if he had been loud and angry.

Still, she felt new respect for him, so she tried to be as honest and thorough as possible. Now was not the time to hold back. She told him everything...about Bo, his computer, what she'd found, the van outside her home, the phone calls, how she'd known she had to leave, all the while fighting feelings of betrayal and fear.

She shook her head. "All I wanted to do was help Bo. It wasn't just that he was such a loner, but that his being alone even excluded God. I couldn't imagine how anybody got through the day, every day, without ever having the presence of our loving Father."

"For some people it just never comes up. Now tell me again how you found the stuff on his computer."

"That's one of those things you're just going to have to take on faith." Bree shrugged. "I could explain it to you half a dozen times, and you still wouldn't make sense out of it. Let's just say I was repairing his hard drive, and these huge encoded cache files kept popping up. I didn't pay much attention at first. I don't usually go snooping in people's stuff while I'm fixing their equipment."

"A good policy. Why didn't you keep to it this time?"

Bree made a wry face. "I wish I had. I've wished that ever since I opened one of those files and all the monsters flew out."

"But you couldn't close the box again, could you, Pandora?" Cody's murmured question brought quick tears to her eyes.

"No." The admission still hurt as much as it had in Indiana.

Cody sighed. "Tell me you went to the police with all this. Maybe even the FBI." He looked at her sharply and frowned. Bree felt transparent under his unnerving gaze. It wasn't a comfortable feeling. "You couldn't do it, could you?"

"I wanted to at first. I paced and thought and prayed for a long time. There just had to be another answer than turning someone I thought was a friend over to the police." Bree looked up at him. She desperately wanted this conversation to end but knew she had to go on. Right now she needed a break. "Can we get a drink someplace? I am so thirsty."

"We need to. I'm thirsty too. Let's grab something from the first convenience store we come to, then keep talking," he said. "This can't wait another day, or even another hour."

"It really can't." Bree laid her hand on Cody's arm. "Because the man I saw today was Bo. And I'm pretty sure he wants to kill me." Cody's eyes blazed in reaction to her statement. Bree had never seen him so angry. Until today she had thought of him as a man who might not be happy a lot, but was even-tempered otherwise. His reactions as she told him about Bo were proof that there was a person behind Cody North's facade that she knew nothing about.

This side of Cody was probably what someone he'd arrested years ago had seen. His golden brown eyes weren't sparkling anymore. Instead they had narrowed, glaring at her. The skin around them crinkled a little, and his dark brows were low and knit.

The frown on his face looked permanent. Bree couldn't imagine finding anything to say that would make him smile at her again. What felt worst was that the trust and openness she'd felt building were gone. His expression was more sober than the night they'd met on the beach, and much less friendly.

"Well, say something, Cody. I thought you would have thought what I did was ingenious. I thought it was. I never imagined Bo knew enough about computers to realize that I'd rigged his hard drive to sabotage his files the first time he opened them."

Cody shook his head. "I'm still not believing all this. Do you realize how stupid some of your choices have been?" His hand came down hard on the picnic table between them. It startled Bree so much she jumped. "No, scratch that. Do you realize how foolish virtually *all* your choices have been in dealing with this guy?"

"Hey, it's never bothered me to be foolish, if I thought it was the right thing," Bree argued. "We're supposed to be fools for Christ all the time."

Cody went livid. "Fools for Christ is one thing. Just plain *foolish* is another prospect altogether. Bree, there was nothing right or godly about what you did. You may have convinced yourself that there was, but even as far away as I stand from God right now, I can see that this isn't what he'd have you do."

Bree's head was spinning. She could feel her pulse racing and the emotion welling up inside, threatening to overwhelm her. Was Cody right? Had she just been fooling herself? She'd thought she was doing the right thing in God's eyes—or had she? Had she just been giving in to fear all this time…just running away?

Oh no. Please, God, have I been that far off?

She shook her head. No, she couldn't believe it. Couldn't think it. Cody had to be wrong. He was just trying to push his ideas and attitudes on her. And he didn't have the right. "How can you say that?"

Tears sprang to her eyes, and she trembled. Who was Cody to tell her what to do? How could he judge her actions and feelings like this?

"I can say that easily. Bree, even I know God directs us to do what is right. He leads us to do it, he wants us to do it, and he supports us when we do it. Can you honestly say you've felt led by the Lord to pull these crazy stunts instead of calling the police on this character?"

Bree felt her face flush even deeper, and she couldn't control the tears any longer. "I thought I felt led that way. But now…" She met his gaze. "Am I absolutely positive I was doing God's will in this? No, probably not. I couldn't turn Bo in. There's good inside him, Cody, I know there is. But I couldn't just sit there in

Indiana and act like bait. Because if I had stayed he would have come after me, making things even worse."

"So you ran. You went over a thousand miles to get away from some lunatic that you're convinced has a good heart under a layer of hate and illegal activity." Cody's words were clipped, measured. Their precision made Bree ache even more. "You run directly into my complex full of people on vacation. You keep three small children with you while you're pretty sure you're being stalked by a maniac."

The force of Cody's anger overwhelmed Bree. "It wasn't like that! At least that wasn't the way I thought about it. I didn't think Bo would come this far after me. And unless I got on the Internet or gave away my location to somebody we both knew, I didn't see how he could find me. It's not like I knew anybody here or had ever talked about going here."

"No; that little you had in your favor. You at least weren't predictable when you ran. But Bree, running isn't ever the answer. It just removes you from your problems for a little while, but they come back. You've been trying to tell me that the whole time you've been on Sanibel. If it works that way for me, it has to work that way for you, too."

"There's some differences here, Cody." Bree stood up and pushed away from the table. It was hard to rise gracefully from a picnic bench. She got both legs over the bench without tripping and started to walk away. "I never left God behind. I still did what I thought he wanted me to, and I'm still trusting him with my care."

"It's a good thing you're trusting somebody, because I sure don't feel like you trusted me," Cody called from his seat at the table. Bree was half a block away before he caught up to her and put a hand on her shoulder.

"You should have trusted me, Bree." He stopped her movement. "Now we're really in a mess. We've got a guy who's probably armed and definitely dangerous chasing after you. Meanwhile, Marisa and the kids and Shawn are at the end of the parade route waiting for us to pick them up. If you go with me to do that, I have to worry about Bo finding everybody. If you don't go with me, I can't be sure you'll do the right thing and talk to the police today about this. And I'll worry about you every minute you're out of my sight."

Bree let go, and tears coursed down her cheeks. "I'm sorry. You're right, I've made one mistake after another. I still don't think I should have gone straight to the police. But maybe I should've stayed in Indiana and talked to Bo."

"At the very least you should have told me what was happening the night I picked you up." Cody's grip on her shoulder didn't let up. Normally Bree would have welcomed his touch, but this time it felt hard and unyielding, the way his eyes looked. "Things would have been easy to fix then. As is, it's a mess. Nothing he's done so far is illegal. The guy can follow you and look at you forever if he doesn't make a move to harm you. And since you rigged his hard drive, the evidence the police would have needed isn't there for them, either."

"Oh yes, it is," Bree said. "I'm not that dumb. I backed everything up before I changed his programs. That's probably why Bo is chasing me in the first place. He hasn't found anybody capable of undoing what I did."

Cody's eyes widened in disbelief. "You have copies of all that evidence? With you *here?* And you still haven't told me about it? Where is it?"

"In a safe place. One where nobody, including Bo, is going to find it."

"No more games." Cody released her shoulder, even though he looked as if he'd rather shake it instead. "When we get back to the complex, you're showing me where everything is. Then we're going to call my buddies on the force and do what you should have done in the first place."

"Okay. I'll at least show you where everything is, but I think it would be better if we didn't call the police on Sanibel."

"If you'd rather call the feds, that would be okay

too," Cody said. He looked noncommittal. Bree felt disappointed. Couldn't he tell her right now that he cared for her? He'd talked about being worried about Marisa and the kids, and Shawn. But where was his concern for her? Apparently he was only worried about losing track of her before she talked to the police. Right now all she felt was stupid.

"I don't want to call anybody. But I will. And it probably should be the police in Indiana where this whole thing started. And where I ought to head back and settle things once and for all." Inside she was still pleading to see some concern from Cody. It wasn't what she got.

"Fine. Have it your way." Cody strode past her, looking ahead on the path. "Right now we have hot, tired children and a woman in a full leg cast to rescue from an asphalt parking lot. It's probably going to take the rest of the afternoon to get everybody home, cooled down, and calmed. We can talk after that."

Bree could only nod silently and follow him. Of all the ways she had expected the parade to end, this had not been among them. Any chances she had of staying on Sanibel Island and getting to know Cody better evaporated before her eyes in the ramrod stiffness of his back.

Have I really strayed that far from what you wanted me to do, Lord? What Bo did was wrong; I know that. But maybe what I've done has been almost as bad.What do I do now? She followed Cody, still listening for an answer that was not coming. Her new life was collapsing in front of her, walking farther away with every purposeful stride Cody made in front of her down the path to the park-ing lot.

Fourteen

FUSSY THREE-YEAR-OLDS AND THEIR WILTED MOTHERS demand a lot of attention. Bree knew in principle that was so, but she learned just how true that was when she and Cody got back to the parking lot. Everybody was mad at her.

Bree didn't think it was possible to feel worse about the day's events than she already did. Once Carlos scowled at her with his fists bunched on his hips, she felt worse. "Where were you? We've been waiting a long time," he told her.

His mother shushed him, but not very loudly. Bree could see that she was as hot and tired as the kids were. Bree started to apologize, but before she could say anything, Charlotte bustled up, looking almost as out of sorts as Carlos.

"I don't know what you were doing, Bree, but it's not good to leave somebody in a cast out in the heat this long," Charlotte chided her. "Ed and I will take Marisa and the little ones back to the complex while you all get things loaded on the truck and follow us."

She didn't leave any room for argument, so Bree didn't give her any. Charlotte was sunburned across her nose to a degree that almost matched her hot pink top. Given her mood on top of it, Bree wasn't surprised that the older woman didn't notice she had been crying. Even if she had noticed and asked, Bree didn't know what she'd tell her. So she just thanked Charlotte for helping out and silently helped Cody and Shawn get the surrey on the back of the truck.

Shawn sensed the mood of the two of them and didn't even bother asking to drive the truck home. He sat between Bree and Cody and said very little on the way. Bree was thankful for his presence between them so that no part of her body would accidentally touch Cody's. Ordinarily she would have craved that innocent contact, but not right now. His tense muscles looked like coiled springs. There was even one place in the plane of his cheek that seemed to jump occasionally. With Shawn in the truck, Cody couldn't continue their discussion. For now that was a good thing as far as Bree was concerned.

"I'll take this back to Mel's once we get it undeco-

rated," Shawn said when they had gotten the pedal surrey back off the truck at Island Breeze. "Do you think
Carlos and Ana will want to help me?"

"They might." Cody shut the tailgate. "How about
you all go inside for a while first and have something to
drink. Then I'll put this thing close to one of the lawn
sprinklers and get the kids to put on swimsuits. You can
kill two birds with one stone and rinse it off while
you're getting it ready to take back to Mel."

If they'd both been in better moods, Bree would
have complimented Cody on his ingenuity. It wasn't
the kind of idea he would usually come up with on his
own. Shawn nodded and left, while the two of them
stood watching him. Neither of them made a move to
go inside where all the sane people were on this hot
July afternoon.

"I've been around you too long," Cody said softly.
"See, I'm starting to come up with things for the kids
to do that are fun. Scary, huh?"

"Not really. You're a creative, fun person someplace inside, Cody. It's just a matter of finding the key
to unlock that side of your personality."

Cody turned to face her. His gaze was still serious
and downcast. "I thought you were that key, Bree. At
least I did until today. Now I'm not so sure."

Bree looked at the gravel under their feet. She
couldn't stand looking into Cody's face with his

wounded expression and know she'd put that expression there. "I understand that. If you want me to leave quickly, I will. I can be gone tomorrow if you like." Saying that tore at her, but maybe things would be better this way.

She'd miss everything and everyone here so much. Shawn and Charlotte and Marisa and the kids had become closer than most of her friends in Indiana. She'd lived there for years but hadn't found the kind of ties there that she'd found on the island. She belonged here; she knew it. God may not have called her to leave Indiana and hide from Bo, but Bree was sure God had a hand in leading her to this place.

Most of all she would miss Cody. She had come to depend on his strength. With him around she didn't fear anything, even being pursued by Bo. Cody brought her down to earth when she needed to be pulled out of her frequent flights of fancy. It felt good being around Cody North in a way she had never felt around any other man. Until today Bree would have said that God had not only led her to Sanibel Island, but to Cody as well.

Had she fouled up God's plan for her life with her stupid decisions on her own? Bree bit her bottom lip, waiting for Cody's answer to her offer to leave. It was slow in coming. Bree could hear cars on the road, horns honking, even the surf of high tide somewhere behind them.

"I can't let you do that, Bree."

Her heart leaped. Couldn't let her do that? Why? Was it because he cared…didn't want her to go? She looked up at him, but his expression was neutral.

He went on. "It sounds attractive in some ways, but it would be dangerous. I don't think Bo is watching this place closely enough to know if you left. He'd still come here and make trouble, and there are just too many people here for that to happen. As it is I'm thinking of calling Harry and asking for a more frequent patrol past the complex any time it's dark."

Bree's heart sank again. Of course. If she left it would interfere with his peaceful, well-ordered life and the safety of his guests. *Well, fine. It's what I deserve after what I've done.* "All right. Do you want me to ask Marisa if the kids want to help Shawn with the surrey?"

Cody shook his head. "I'll do it myself. Maybe later when you've had some time to think, and I have too, we'll talk. I'll see you this evening, all right?"

"Sure." She turned and walked away from Cody, walking fast so he didn't see that she was crying again.

"I may cry all night," she told Gabe a couple of hours later. She'd taken a shower and thrown everything in the dirty clothes basket into the washing machine. There wasn't much else to pack up. And no matter what Cody said, Bree was determined to pack up. She'd find a way to lessen the danger for the others in the complex if she left. Bree just didn't know how she could bear staying for a long, drawn-out good-bye that would tear her to pieces.

How was she going to explain to Sarita that she was leaving and wouldn't ever see her again? What would happen with Marisa once the cast came off? Would Cody keep softening his anger and frustration and come back into God's presence the way Bree had felt him start to do? Not knowing any of those things would be devastating.

Bree felt very strongly, though, that Cody was right about one thing. She needed to make things right, with God and with the authorities. Making things right with the authorities would be easier in Indiana. Perhaps this painful leave-taking was the consequence of her mad flight down here in the first place.

"No!" Bree put down the shirt she was folding into a suitcase. She said it so loudly it startled Gabe. He jumped straight up from giving himself a thorough bath while lying on the lid of the suitcase. Staring at her, he made noises in his throat then stalked off to some calmer place to finish his bath.

"I'm sorry, Gabriel. Guess I was thinking out loud. But I don't think that's how God works. Cody's right; running down here wasn't the thing to do. I should have at least called the police and given them Bo's disks before I left, if I felt I had to leave. Now I'm stuck down here when I should be there. And I don't really want to see Indiana again."

Yorktown had bad memories for her now. Bree wondered how many other people had taken advantage of her trusting nature. She'd never looked at life that way before, but thanks to Bo and Cody it was becoming habit now.

What would she do in Yorktown? Compared to Sanibel her life up north was flat. She missed her church friends, but after a couple of weeks at Island Community she was already making friends here that meant as much to her. That was something that had taken months in Indiana. Here people were used to folks coming and going, and as a result most of them offered friendship easily.

Bree stood in the middle of her room, still over the suitcase, and thought about people back in Indiana. She tried to think of one person that she missed enough to talk to in Yorktown. A scruffy image came to mind. "Scooter!" Picking up the phone, she dialed his number. It would probably be busy because he only had one phone line, and he was almost always on the computer.

What happened instead startled her. A three-toned beep came on the line, followed by an operator's recorded message. "The number you have dialed is no longer in service. The new number is unpublished at the request of the holder." Scooter with an unlisted number? That didn't make a whole lot of sense.

Hanging up the phone, Bree got cold chills up the back of her neck. Something Scooter had said online last week came back to her. He'd gotten a hacking job so big he could afford to go to the nearby state college. Bree could only think of a few people that had enough money to pay for something like that, and Scooter would have mentioned if he were working for one of the businesses in town. "Dear Lord, please protect Scooter. Don't let him have suffered because of what I've done." Because suddenly she knew where Scooter had gotten his windfall of money. It could only be Bo, and Bo wasn't good about paying honest debts.

The phone in the office was busy. Cody hung up his kitchen phone and thought about marching across the asphalt to confront Bree. He hadn't said nearly all of what he wanted to yet. He had several things to tell her about how irresponsible she had been coming down here and making a mess of his life. He also had to thank her for coming down here and making a mess of his life, which he had neglected to say anything about in his anger.

He'd never been good at expressing his feelings, and being a police officer hadn't made things easier. Having Dave die suddenly on him had made things even worse. There was still so much, to this day, that Cody wished he'd told Dave. If he didn't watch it, he was going to find himself in a similar situation with Bree. True, she'd still be alive, but she would go back home to Indiana without his ever telling her how he felt. The only alternative was pursuing her to Indiana, and that wasn't likely. How could he leave a thriving business and a teenager long enough to traipse across the country? Not even for Bree. He would have to tell her in person if he was going to tell her at all.

It wasn't going to happen on the phone tonight, anyway. The line was still busy. He didn't know what he would say when he went over and knocked on the door, but it had to be done. If he didn't go over soon, Bree would think that the only thing he felt toward her was anger. That was far from the truth, even though he'd been a Neanderthal about expressing himself earlier.

He replayed the scene in his head, wincing at some of the things he'd said to Bree. Why hadn't he told her that he was worried mainly because the thought of her pitting herself against someone like Bo terrified him? That she was far too sweet and trusting to try to take on someone who thought that guns were toys and that people—if they didn't agree with him—weren't very worthwhile and were expendable. Why hadn't he come right out and told her how important she was to him, even if he was mad at her?

Sure, he was angry that she had made a bad judgement call about involving him and the Montoya family without their knowledge. If he'd known about this character, Cody was sure he could have gotten him arrested in Indiana someplace. Especially if they had those disks that Bree told him were in a safe place. With a personality like hers, heaven only knew what she considered a safe place. That was the second most important thing Cody kicked himself over not bringing up.

It was time to go over and talk to Bree. Everything was fairly quiet in the complex. There were people having a Fourth of July party around the pool deck, but it was a peaceful event. The day had been so hot that the few folks who often gathered around the hot tub once it got dark and got raucous didn't want to be in the hot water. In a few hours the fireworks would start out on Tarpon Bay, and everyone would be watching that. Maybe by then he and Bree could mend their differences and take a blanket and plenty of bug repellent down to the beach. Fourth of July fireworks made a good background for fixing arguments and making declarations of love, didn't they?

Cody headed to the kitchen door. There was a tiny shriek when he opened it. "I didn't knock yet," Ana said, looking like a startled forest creature. "How did you know I was here?"

"I didn't." The kid looked frazzled. "What's the matter?"

"Mama needs help. Carlito threw up, and we don't have anything to settle his stomach. Mama says he's just hot and excited from the Fourth and everything, but the soda machine down by the pool won't take my money, and I can't get anything for him, and he thinks he's going to do it again. And Mama says she can't chase after Sarita when she's well and Carlos when he's sick and..." Her deep brown eyes were filled with tears.

"I get the picture. Give me a minute to gather up a few things and I'll be right there, okay, Ana?" Bree would have to wait. Marisa Montoya needed him more right now. Maybe once he got over there he would send Ana over to get Bree as well. They couldn't solve any of their differences while nursing a sick kid, but at least they'd be together. "Have you tried Bree?"

Ana nodded. "She didn't come to the door when I knocked. She said from inside that she needed to be alone and asked me to come back later."

It sounded odd to Cody, out of character for Bree, but she was entitled to be out of sorts tonight. He'd go over and help Marisa, then on his way home he'd stop and talk to Bree. Right now Ana was dancing at the doorway, anxious for him to follow her. "Let me get something to settle Carlos's stomach and a few other things. Tell your mom I'll be there in a minute."

Ana dashed off while Cody rummaged around the kitchen. It wasn't going to be the evening he'd planned, but then nothing about this day had gone as planned, so why should the evening be any different?

He went to the refrigerator. "Great, Shawn. You have to get all teenaged on me right now, don't you?" he asked the empty air, looking at the virtually empty two-liter soda bottle in the refrigerator. "Let me guess. We're out of ice, too." He opened the freezer. There were three lonely cubes at the bottom of the ice holder. Shawn had said he was taking a few things over to his friend's house for their party. Why hadn't Cody paid more attention?

There was more ice out in the freezer in the garage. And more soda out there on the shelves, ready to go into the machine. It would do in a pinch. Cody sighed and headed toward the door. It was definitely going to be a very long evening.

"That was very good, Bree." Bo's voice was low and even——and made the hair on Bree's neck stand on end. "I liked the way you told her to come back later. You don't think she suspected anything, do you?"

"She's a little kid." Bree tried not to look at the semiautomatic pistol he had pointed at her. "She doesn't suspect anything. She probably just wanted to come in and watch cable with me."

"You, turning into a couch potato and baby-sitter? It boggles the mind." His silky voice made her shiver. How could he be so cool and collected while breaking into her apartment and threatening to shoot her? Bo got up off the arm of the sofa and moved his considerable bulk to the sliding glass door. He looked out without disturbing the vertical blinds. "Nobody out there right now. It would be a good time for us to leave, I think."

"Leave? But you just got here." Bree struggled to keep the hysteria out of her voice. If they left now, she wasn't going to have any way to get a message to Cody, to let him know what was going on.

"I certainly did. And I don't want to stay too long. Someone might notice me, and I can't imagine that you haven't told your friends about the sinister figure you saw at the parade today. Am I right?"

"They know." Bree glared at Bo. "Which is why you'll be in even more trouble if you take me away from here. Kidnapping is a federal offense."

"Only if you get caught." Bo waved the short barrel of his gun in her direction. "And I have absolutely no intention of getting caught. Now get up slowly and come over here. We have a little trip to make."

"Where are you taking me?" She didn't expect an answer, but it ate up a little more time. Time that would

allow Cody to look for her, or someone from the complex to come to the office and interrupt this nightmare.

"Away." Bo motioned with the gun. "Someplace
where you can think. I wonder, should I prove to you
that I mean business before we leave? I could use that
stupid cat for target practice on the way out—"

"No!" Bree moved to protect Gabe, and all the
people in the complex as well. Bo meant business.
"Let's just go." She was going to have to trust God for
her safety and go with this monster. It was the hardest
thing she had ever done. But the thought of any of the
Montoyas or Shawn or even Cody walking in on an
armed Bo made her move fast. It was time to put them
out of harm's way, even if she paid for it with her life.

Fifteen

CARLOS MONTOYA SAT ON THE COUCH, WATCHING A video. He looked far healthier than he had when Cody came over. "*Gracias* for your help," Marisa said, pushing a lock of hair off her damp forehead. "We have been much trouble."

"Not that much trouble," Cody said. "And I really feel like I brought this trouble on myself. If I'd found a way to communicate with you, the accident would not have happened."

Marisa shook her head. "Bree said the same thing. I told her she was wrong. God has us in his hands, Señor North. He keeps me under his wings, even in cast." Her smile was brilliant. Cody wished again that he had the belief that she and Bree did—that God was there for him personally.

"How can you say that? You're out of work, injured, your husband is..." Cody stalled. He wasn't sure how much the children knew.

"In prison. They know where he is; at least Ana does. Carlito pretends he doesn't, Sarita does not understand," Marisa told him. "We have told them truth, that Papa made bad mistakes and must...pay price." Ana was there, standing beside her mother. "Even God makes clear that our actions have..." Marisa looked up at Ana and said a phrase in Spanish. Ana supplied the right word in English, and Marisa repeated it. "They have consequences. That does not mean God has gone away."

Cody swallowed hard. She made everything sound so simple. Perhaps that was his problem, that he refused to let things be simple when they could be. "You don't know how you help me, Marisa. And please, call me Cody instead of Señor North, okay?"

"If you wish. Did you ever reach Bree by phone?"

Cody shook his head. "Busy every time I tried. Maybe she wants to be alone tonight, like she told Ana. I'll let her be until morning." He pointed to the screened-in porch on the back of the unit. "You should be able to see the fireworks from there in a very short time. I'll check in tomorrow morning to see how things are. Good night."

"Good night," Marisa and Ana chorused. Ana let

Cody out, and he walked to the house.

So much for his grand plans to go out and watch the fireworks on the beach with Bree and make a few fireworks of their own. For a moment he considered going over and banging on the door until she came and answered it. He ached to make things right between them, to tell Bree all the things he had left unsaid before. The urge was so strong he started toward her apartment. Then, with a muttered exclamation, he changed direction and went back to his own kitchen door.

Bree wanted to be alone, and for a change he'd honor her wishes. Morning would be soon enough to talk to her again, if she would even talk to him. Cody headed indoors, feeling tired.

A fitful night's sleep didn't help his disposition in the morning. Shawn had made his curfew, just barely. He followed standard procedure of waking Cody up to prove he'd gotten in on time. Usually that would have thrilled Cody silly, but this time he'd just gotten to sleep and it took hours to relax enough to go back. Every little noise—the air-conditioning cycling on and off, the predawn seabirds—brought him to the surface of his rocky sleep.

Finally it was six in the morning, broad daylight, and he was in the kitchen having coffee. "I don't care if she does want to sleep in." Cody set his cup down with

227

a thud. "I'm going over there and we're going to talk." He considered pouring a second mug of coffee and taking them both over to the apartment behind the office as a sort of peace offering. But then he realized he'd never seen Bree, even in the morning, dive for the coffeepot the way he did. She was sunny and cheerful without caffeine first thing in the morning.

So he walked across the crushed-shell parking lot with empty hands and began to tap on the sliding glass door. It was only a few feet from that foldout sofa bed. How could she sleep through the noise? Bree had to be ignoring him. Cody tapped harder and got a shock. The glass door moved under his hand, sliding open a crack. This was wrong. Even Bree didn't leave her door unlocked.

His concern grew when he called into the space and no one answered. Gabe came straight to the glass door and looked up at him. *"Rrowwl?"* It was a concerned sort of sound, and one that echoed Cody's own growing sense of alarm. Pushing the door open, he went into Bree's apartment. He and Gabe were definitely the only occupants.

The door between the office and the apartment was open. "I don't like the looks of this." There was nothing really out of place in the apartment except an open suitcase looking half packed. Cody considered that Bree might've just taken a break in the middle of packing to go and walk on the beach. That would explain the unlocked door. It wouldn't explain the open door to the office.

The phone on the counter was off the hook. So that was why it had rung busy all evening. Cody was getting more and more concerned. It wasn't like Bree to shut everybody out for this long. She wouldn't leave the complex phone off the hook, not even for an hour, let alone all night. Cody could see her getting caught up in something with the computer and staying on the line for hours, but not just leaving the phone off the hook.

He looked around the office. Nothing else looked strange except one drawer partly open. It was the drawer Charlotte locked at night, and it seemed to be forced open. Nothing had been taken that he could determine, not even the ten dollars of petty cash Charlotte kept there.

Cody went to the front door of the office. He found it still locked, as it should be. Through the glass he saw something that disturbed him more than anything he had seen so far. Bree's car was still where she'd parked it two days ago. Her suitcase was out, Gabe was still here, the computer was plugged in just the way he'd expect it, but Bree was gone.

A thump on the countertop next to him startled Cody. Soft white paws climbed his chest as Gabe

229

reached up, standing on his hind legs and walking up Cody with his front paws, yowling insistently. He wasn't happy and he wanted attention. And probably food, judging from the insistence of his pawing.

That clinched things for Cody. Bree wouldn't leave the complex without feeding her cat. No way. Not unless—

Cody clenched his jaw. Not unless she'd had no choice. About feeding the cat. About leaving the complex.

He headed for the phone. It was time to call Harry and make things official. Bree Trehearn was a missing person, and Cody didn't like the way things were headed.

The little room Bree was in was hot and sticky. A feeble air conditioner ran part of the time, but not enough to do much good. "My room is nice and cool." Bo sneered at her. "I'd be happy to let you go over there if you'd just tell me how to retrieve my property."

Sure he would. Bree didn't trust a word that came out of Bo's mouth anymore. After riding around in the dark last night, her hands bound together with duct tape and her body stretched out in the backseat of his car, she was thoroughly disoriented. She had no idea where the shack he'd marched her into was located. It had to be on Sanibel or Captiva, the sister island connected by a roadway, because Bree knew they hadn't gone over the causeway to the mainland.

That still left a lot of territory and no way to get a message to Cody. The room where she sat captive was little more than a cell. It had no windows, and the air-conditioning unit protruded from one cinder-block wall. Even if she could get the tape off her hands fast enough to do something, there was no way out except the door to Bo's adjoining room.

She didn't have the strength to push the air conditioner out through its wall opening, and the adjoining bathroom cubicle only had a solid glass-block window. A sagging couch that looked as if some earlier occupant had rescued it from a junk heap was the only furniture. She was thirsty and hungry. "Hot, tired, hungry, thirsty," Bree whispered to herself. "But not alone." God was here with her, and he'd get her through this. She hadn't stopped praying since Bo marched her out to his nondescript rental car.

As if God had heard her needs the moment they were spoken and decided to act on them, the door opened and Bo came in with a tall container of bottled water.

"I'll be nice and let you have this." He thrust it at Bree's hands, still taped together in front of her. "And then you'll be nice to me afterward, won't you, Bree? We need to talk about my missing property. Our little talk can go easy or it can go rough. It's all up to you."

Bree took the water, drinking quickly. The cool liquid felt wonderful on her dry throat. If she had been alone, she would have wiped the bottle over her brow to cool herself down as well. With Bo in the room she didn't want him to see any more of her discomfort than she had to reveal. "I don't intend to talk, Bo." She willed her voice not to quiver. "Cody's going to find me soon, and this will all be over."

"Not likely, Trehearn." Bo directed an icy glare her way. "I didn't leave any trail to this place and we weren't followed. Nobody is going to find us unless I want them to. Now you need to tell me where my files are. Then we can go home."

"I don't think so. I know more about you than you want me to. What did you do with Scooter?" She knew the question would get a reaction out of him.

Bo's scowl cut a channel in his brow. "Scooter was unfortunate. He just couldn't leave things alone. He refused to accept my simple explanation as to why I wanted to track you to wherever you'd gone. I don't think he'll be attending State in the fall as he'd hoped."

"You...you *killed* him?" Bree's voice was little more than a squeak.

"Oh no. That would be far too messy. But he does understand that crossing me again would be a very poor idea," Bo said, much too smoothly for Bree's comfort. "I hope you understand it as well. I need my information back, Bree. Once I get it, I'll be going. Won't that be more comfortable for all of us?"

"More comfortable for you. I wouldn't be very comfortable with myself if I just let you have that stuff back."

Bo grabbed the water bottle. "Well, you won't be very comfortable soon if you don't tell me where it is, Bree. I'll give you another hour in here to think about things. Then maybe you'll be ready to talk."

He left the room, shutting the door behind him. With the door shut again the room got warm quickly. Bree could feel her throat going dry. She was close to panic. Bree wished she'd done more Bible memorization. Knowing as much of God's Word as possible would be a comfort right now.

As if on command, a verse she'd almost forgotten slipped into her memory. Where was it from? Someplace in Paul's letters to Timothy, she was pretty sure. After she got out of this nasty little room, the first time she got her hands on a Bible she would find out. For now it was enough to run it through her mind, not knowing exactly where it was in Scripture. "For God did not give us a spirit of timidity, but a spirit of power, of love and of a sound mind." She needed all those things right now. These were promises she needed to claim. And there was no time like the present. It didn't seem nearly as hot in the room as Bree began claiming her promises.

Harry looked up from the countertop in the office at Island Breeze. "You're sure about what you've told us? That your friend Bree was abducted by this guy, whoever he is, and it happened here in the last twelve hours?"

"Positive. Have you ever had reason to doubt me before?"

"No, but if this guy was in here, he was good. No sign of forced entry, no prints on the computer or phone that shouldn't be here, nothing."

"If what Bree told me about him is true, he could be that good. I am really worried, Harry."

"We'll do what we can. I'll run the information you gave me on the national network and see if we can come up with a possible last location. And I'll call the Indiana state police and the locals in that little town you said they were from."

"Yorktown," Cody said. "It's the only town she mentioned, anyway. I'd start looking there for information on this guy. One thing she did tell me—he likes guns. So if you find him, be careful."

"Don't worry about that. I'm always careful. You don't live this long in uniform if you're not."

"Yeah, well, sometimes you don't live that long in uniform even if you are." Cody met Harry's curious glance with a grim shrug. "When this is all over we're going to have to talk."

"I'd like that. You've got some stories to tell after a few years in Tampa, I'm sure. Hang on here, Cody, and don't do anything by yourself. You're not on the force anymore, remember."

"I'll remember." Cody wasn't sure how much he'd remember if Bree's life hung in the balance. If he found himself in a situation where he could either move to find her, or stop and call Harry, but not both, it wouldn't be calling Harry. That just wasn't what first came to mind. Harry didn't need to hear that from him, though.

For now he would do things Harry's way, Cody thought as he walked him to the door and watched him get into his car. How long doing things Harry's way lasted depended on what he found out. Cody paced around the office, looking at everything in a new light.

It was apparent that Bo hadn't found the disks. If he had, Bree wouldn't have been taken. She might be here, dead on the floor, but she wouldn't be gone. Cody shuddered at the thought. Why hadn't he pressed her for an answer? He called himself every name in the book for what he'd done last night.

If he had only gotten over here at the right time,

none of this would've happened. Bree's telling Ana to leave her alone was so foreign to what he knew of her usual behavior. She was always the first to answer the call in a crisis, especially if it involved the kids. The image of what really happened behind her door, with that slimy thug pointing a gun at Bree, made Cody's blood run cold.

On the other hand, he was thankful Bree hadn't let Ana into the apartment. Bo with two hostages wasn't a situation he wanted to think about. This one was bad enough. He had to commend Bree's quick thinking for not letting Ana in. And he had to cite himself for stupidity for not catching on when she sent Ana back to the apartment with a message he should have deciphered.

Where were those disks? He'd looked everyplace in Bree's apartment and the office that made sense to him, and even a few that hadn't. He'd even had Shawn go through all the disks that were in the flip-top box next to the computer, in case Bree had been hiding them in plain sight. There wasn't anything unusual on any of them. This was driving him crazy.

Gabe came strolling into the office.

"So you got out from under the bed, now that everybody strange is gone." Cody checked the cat's food dish. Still full and untouched. "Wish you were a watch cat, or a tracker cat, or something so you could lead me to where he's taken her. Why couldn't Bree have had a bloodhound for a pet instead of a worthless dust mop like you?"

Gabe sat down on the rug and glared at him, looking for all the world as though he understood what Cody was saying. Then he yowled mournfully. "All right, we'll complain together." Cody went to the surprised cat and scooped him up. He didn't stay in Cody's arms long, struggling out after a moment. "Have it your way. I know I'm not as cuddly as Bree, but I thought I'd do in a pinch." Gabe obviously thought otherwise, as he stalked off to find somewhere to sulk. Cody paced around the office again, wishing he could sulk as effectively as the cat. Pacing and worrying weren't getting him anywhere.

What would Bree do if the situation were reversed? Cody snorted. The situation would never be reversed because he had the common sense not to get himself in this kind of situation. But if Bree were alone and worried about him, what would she do? The answer was quick in coming. She would pray.

Praying wasn't Cody's first reaction to a crisis. It wasn't even his second reaction. But it was definitely what Bree would've done. Well, he could pace and pray, couldn't he? "Okay, Lord, I'm rusty at this. But please keep Bree in your care. Guide Harry. Help him and help me, to find Bree before that maniac does something we'll all regret." At this rate he was going to wear a hole in the rug soon. Just pacing back and forth he would have done that anyway. If he prayed while he paced, at least he didn't feel so alone.

Sixteen

"YOU'RE NOT GOING TO LIKE WHAT I HAVE TO TELL YOU," Harry said on the phone.

Unless the news was that he had Bo in custody and Bree safe beside him, Cody knew that was the truth. His eyes were tired and gritty from worry and lack of sleep. "Doesn't sound like it." A tense silence hung between them. "Tell me anyway, so I can at least decide."

"Indiana state police and the Yorktown authorities both know our friend Bo. Harold Bowen is not a nice guy. Several outstanding warrants, including arson for torching a rundown house on the edge of town that housed a computer repair shop—"

Bree's home. It had to be. Cody clenched his jaw. The crumb had torched Bree's house.

"—and another suspicious fire in the car of a junior-college student. Fortunately the student wasn't in it at the time."

"Any convictions?" Cody's throat tightened.

"Weapons stuff as a minor. And some Klan involvement. Apparently there are parts of Indiana that still let our pointy-headed friends flourish, as long as they do it quietly. Lately Bowen seems to be involved in a splinter group that even the Klan won't claim. If this is what Bree was running away from, she did the natural thing, North."

"You're right. But you haven't found any sign of Bowen and Bree on the island, either, or you wouldn't be calling me telling me this."

"True. We've got a search going on neighborhood to neighborhood, making sure nobody knows of any vacation property being broken into or caretakers' houses open when they shouldn't be. And we're canvassing real estate companies to make sure nobody matching Bowen's description has rented a place on a walk-in during the last two weeks. We'll find them," Harry said.

Cody wished that were reassuring. He thanked Harry and hung up. He couldn't just sit in this office and do nothing. There had to be some way to help Bree. The police were doing all they could, legally. But every moment that ticked by worried Cody more.

What was Bree going through? Cody had dealt with creeps like this before. A man like Bowen wouldn't keep her alive unless she fulfilled a purpose. In this case Bree's purpose was getting back the information. Once that was done, her life wouldn't be worth much.

Cody stretched. The office felt too closed in, too air-conditioned and set apart from everybody else. *There has to be something I can do to do to find Bree, or better still, find the disks.* Cody grabbed his sunglasses and a hat and went outside. On the playground in the grass area at the center of the complex, Sarita and Carlos were playing on the swings with two other children.

Cody vaguely remembered the other two. Their mom and dad were from Michigan, and they usually came for a week or two in the summer and stayed in Jacaranda, unit C. Both children were little boys with blond buzz cuts. They and Carlos were being admonished by the boys' father that they couldn't have one of those contests where they jumped off the swings.

"I didn't drive all the way down here to find an emergency room, guys," the father told them. "So no jumping off moving swings, got it? That goes for you too, bud." The father pointed at Carlos. "Your mom doesn't need any more medical trips, either."

"Okay," Carlos said. Sarita was asking for another push. Cody took over that duty—more of a pleasure, really—from the other man.

"Thanks." The man held out his hand. "You're the manager here, aren't you?"

Cody returned his handshake. "Manager and part owner. Cody North. Anything I can do for you?" He didn't really feel like dealing with anybody else's problems right now, but it was part of his job whether he felt up to it or not. And it might take his mind off his troubles.

"No problems. I'm Ken Stevenson. We're in Jacaranda C. Just wondered where the new office person was. The blonde with the unusual name. She and my wife had made some kind of plans to go to the outlet mall before we went home, and I haven't seen her around in a couple days."

"That's Bree. And she had a little family emergency and had to leave for a while." Cody pushed Sarita's swing. "We're hoping she comes back soon."

"Mama is helping us pray for her, and for the policemen," Carlos piped up, making Cody wince.

Ken's forehead crinkled. "Police? Is there something wrong?"

"Well, Bree did have an emergency, but it wasn't related to family." Cody hadn't wanted to tell any of the guests the truth. No sense in alarming them. But thanks to Carlos, he didn't have much of a choice this time. "She's been missing for over a day now."

"Missing? Do other people here know about this?" Ken asked.

"No, and I'd appreciate it if we kept it that way. I don't want anyone getting alarmed."

"They'd be more alarmed if they knew Bree was missing and nobody was told," Ken said. "Do you know she was getting Bible study groups going around the pool? And she introduced us to this great couple from Munich and we've been having the best time. We might even plan a house swap next year."

Bree had worked her magic everywhere, it seemed. "So you think it would be a good idea to tell people about Bree?"

Ken nodded. "As long as you can do it quietly, yes. I don't have any talents that would help me search for her, but I could start a prayer chain of people to ask for guidance for the searchers and help for Bree, wherever she is."

Cody swallowed hard. Even with Bree gone, God was still finding ways to reach out to him through other people. "That would be great. I'll have Charlotte call the guests and tenants so we can talk to everybody. Maybe this afternoon before the talk on shells, at the pavilion?"

Ken agreed. "That would help. And thanks for pushing Sarita for a while. That little kid is solid." Sarita giggled and leaned her head back.

"Push more. Push harder," she shrieked in glee. Cody had to go along with Ken. Sarita was solid, and enthusiastic about everything. It was good to take his mind off his worries by pushing her in the swing.

The swing set had been part of the complex before Cody took it over. He marveled again at the craftsmanship someone had used with metal pipe and cedar to make a frame that withstood this much pressure. Hundreds of kids had played on the unit and still it stood firm.

Just like the framework I've built in you, a quiet voice deep inside reminded him. He almost vaulted Sarita into space, so great was his surprise. He wasn't sure if he had ever heard God speak to him directly. He focused on Sarita's back, swinging her again. He watched his hands reach out and clasp the swing firmly, curling in to hold the trunk of her small body as well. Just as he was in God's hands...as he had always been.

Cody considered himself a strong man. But it was all he could do not to stagger and fall to his knees. He was in God's presence. Right here. Right now. He knew it as certainly as he knew his own name. The God of the universe was here, with him, Cody North. He was all around him and within him, speaking to him...caring about him...letting Cody know he wasn't alone.

His breath caught on a ragged sob. *Jesus...Jesus, forgive me.*

He had been envying Bree her relationship with God the whole time she was at Island Breeze. She kept trying to tell him that the same kind of personal walk with Jesus was right in front of him, that all he had to do was take it.

Now here it was, real and concrete, in front of him as clearly as Sarita's laughing form in her little red shorts set. "Yes," he whispered. Goose bumps rose on his arms with the awareness of God's holy presence. Cody knew he wasn't deserving, couldn't ever be…but that didn't matter. God was there. For him. His spirit soared, stealing his breath away, as he felt his heart open. "Please. Work in me." Still standing there, pushing Sarita on the swing set, Cody had to use one hand to backhand tears from his face. He looked around the yard. He could hear gulls and the surf, children laughing and their parents calling them. Funny, it didn't look at all like the road to Damascus. It just looked like another normal day at Island Breeze.

But Cody knew different. And he knew nothing about him…about *life*…was going to be the same.

Bo opened the door. "So, are we going to talk this time?" I've got dinner in here and a cold glass of beer. Aren't you hungry and thirsty?"

"You know I am." Bree was too hot and tired to put

on her usual brave front. "Why ask?"

"Just making sure you knew it too. You're far too noble, Bree." Bo lounged in the doorway. "Why don't you just tell me where my property is so that we can end this farce? The holiday weekend is almost over, and I need to be getting back to Indiana."

"You're not going back up to Indiana or anywhere close, Bo." Bree tried to sound as sure of herself as possible. "Unless it's to a federal prison cell."

"Very funny. Nobody has any way to prove I've committed a crime worthy of federal prison, Bree. Nobody except you, perhaps. And you won't be telling anybody about me."

A chill ran up her spine, replacing the trickle of sweat that soaked her shirt. It couldn't get any clearer than that. Bo didn't intend to leave her alive, whether she told him about the disks or not.

"How do you know that?" She wondered if he would really tell her what he planned to do.

"I know you, Bree. I thought I did before, but I was wrong. Tracking you, watching you here on the island confirmed most of what I thought I knew. You may think you're brave and self-reliant, but you have your soft spots. And if you don't cooperate soon, I'm going to start probing those soft spots one by one." Bo's voice was silky, in a menacing way. "Nobody knew I went in and out of that condo complex you were staying at.

Nobody at all. Don't you think I could slip in and out again for a much smaller package? If I could get a full-grown woman out so easily, what's to stop me with a smaller body?"

Bree turned her head. "I love my cat, Bo, but I won't play your game. If I had the information you think I have, I wouldn't trade it for Gabe's comfort. Or even his life."

Bo's laugh dripped with spite. "Oh, not that small a package. I should have just broken his fuzzy neck or shot him when I was there before, to prove to you I meant business. Guess even I have too soft a heart for some things. I was talking about that little kid that follows you around everywhere. The little brat. Her mother must be neglectful, because she lets her run everywhere, you know. The girl would be so easy to pick up. As long as I shut her up. She seems to have the annoying habit of most small children of being loud and obnoxious."

Bree was trying not to show any emotion. "I have no idea what you're talking about."

"You're a bad liar, Bree. You just lost all the color the Florida sunshine has put into your charming cheeks. Yes, that's the answer to my dilemma, isn't it?" There was a touch of wicked glee in his voice. "Just pick up one of the children there. You wouldn't last ten minutes with one of them in front of you, even if I did nothing harsher than—"

"Stop. Don't go on." Bree stared at Bo in numb horror. "I'll tell you where the disks are. But first you have to promise me that if you go back to Island Breeze, all you'll take is those disks."

"That was my original intent. I'd only threatened otherwise because you've been so…difficult," Bo said, softly and slowly. How did anyone so calm put so much menace into his voice? "Now, why don't you start telling me what I need to know."

Forgive me, Father. Bree closed her eyes. *And be with Cody and the Montoyas; protect them from this evil man.* She took a long, deep breath that shuddered through her body. "All right. It's simple, really. Just listen close."

Cody was in the office, sitting in the chair Bree normally sat in. His elbows rested on the counter in front of him; his head was in his hands. Instead of turning the place upside down again, as he'd been tempted to do earlier in the day, he was doing what he should have done all along. He was praying.

He still felt incredibly rusty in this department. The comforting thing was that Cody was sure God didn't mind. That he welcomed the prayers of a sinner returned, even if they weren't very eloquent. "Okay, Lord, I know those disks are here someplace. And I know the information isn't stored in the hard drive of that computer. Shawn's gone through it, Charlotte's gone through it, there's nothing there." Still Cody felt the same message over and over again.

Check the computer. It was as clear as if someone were in the room speaking. He looked at the hunk of metal, plastic, and glass in front of him. He'd done everything he knew how, and the information just wasn't there.

With a whump Gabe's body landed on the countertop. Cody reached out a hand to scratch behind his ears. "It's a shame you can't talk. At least that you can't talk in a way I can understand. Bree seemed to understand you just fine," Cody said. The cat obviously missed Bree. He kept roaming around looking for familiar scents and sounds.

Prowling, Gabe rubbed his jaw against the corner of the monitor. It rotated a little, and Cody put it back into place. "Don't do that. You'll knock something over." The monitor was solid and heavy, frustrating in its silence. Gabe probably couldn't knock it over.

Gabe wasn't finished. He kept after the computer, rubbing his face on the tower now that held the disk drive and CD-ROM. Finally he jumped up on top of the tower. "You aren't going to fit. That's too narrow." Cody lifted him off. His knuckles rapped the case, making a hollow sound. Putting the cat down on the carpet, where he meowed a complaint, Cody went back to the case. He rapped it again, this time on purpose. It made a noise like the Tin Man. "This case is hollow. Is this what 'check the computer' means?"

He moved the case forward, looking at the sides. Rotating it gently, he looked at the back, then the base. Setting it back down, he went for his small office tool kit. It took a few seconds with a small Phillips screwdriver before the metal housing slid away.

Inside was a collection of parts he couldn't identify. There was also one other thing that made his heart leap. Taped to the side of the case was a plastic sandwich bag. And inside the bag were two diskettes.

"All right. This is it." He reached inside to pull the bag out. Putting the computer case back together, he slipped a diskette into the proper slot and opened it on screen. The coded files didn't mean much to him, but he was sure they were Bowen's files.

Taking the disk out of the computer, he slid it back into the plastic bag and reached for the phone to call Harry. Then he hesitated, his hand poised over the phone.

Bowen would come back for this. Cody was sure of it, because he was sure that the man would find a way to get Bree to tell him where the information was. Bowen was evil and Bree was vulnerable. If they wanted to catch Bowen, the way to do it was to set a trap with these disks as bait. Cody looked up at the clock in the office. It was a little after five in the evening. Once it got dark, he suspected that Bowen would be back.

"Harry won't like this." He would want to go through more official channels, stake the place out with half a dozen cops. That would only frighten the man away. If they did that, it might be too late for Bree. It made a lot more sense just to set the trap and wait by himself.

Cody was already going over his plans, taking stock of what kind of firepower he had around the place, and what to wear to be inconspicuous, when it hit him. Guilt. No...that wasn't right. Conviction. Yes. That was it. He was doing something wrong.

Cody rocked back in his chair as if pushed by a giant hand. What was he doing? As much as he hated to admit it, he was using the same crazy logic that had made him so mad at Bree. He and God could handle anything alone, couldn't they? It *did* make perfect sense this way. Limp and shaking, his pulse roared in his ears. Suddenly it was so easy to see how Bree had come to these same conclusions.

He'd railed at her, but when faced with a similar situation, to act alone with God or turn something important over to another authority, Cody chose to do it himself, with God. Just like Bree. She hadn't gone to the cops, either. Like him just now, she'd been sure she and the Lord could handle Harold Bowen.

Sure, God could take care of a two-bit criminal with no trouble, but Cody knew Bree's—and his— plan wasn't right. God wasn't a magic wand to wave over trouble to make it disappear. He'd given people common sense and put authorities in place for a reason.

He was going to have to do a lot more praying, Cody decided as he put the computer case back together, its precious cargo stored inside again just where Bree had left it. "If this is the right thing, done the right way, please make sure it goes according to your plan, Lord."

The cat looked up at him, and if he didn't know better, Cody could have sworn Gabe smiled. Smile or no smile, he was content to curl up and nap in a corner for the first time since Bree had left. If Gabe's actions were any indication, things were going just right. Cody reached for the phone, and this time he punched in Harry's number. Time to get this show on the road. They only had a few hours before the trap would be sprung. That was clear to Cody now. He marveled at the connection he still held with Bree, how he could hardly wait to tell her that her message got through.

He ached to hold her, to take care of her, to rescue her from Bowen. Of course, he also itched to throttle her for getting into this predicament. But he wouldn't give in to those impulses again, no matter how much trouble it took to get Bree back. This time he was going to do things right all the way.

Seventeen

BREE WAS SHIVERING AND SWEATING AT THE SAME TIME. Being cool and comfortable worried her more than being too warm. She didn't know what Bo had in mind, but it couldn't be good. He was still doing something with the bindings at the back of the straight chair in which she sat.

The fact that he'd brought another piece of furniture into her cubicle worried her too. She knew he only did this because she wouldn't be secure enough to suit him on the sofa. Things were moving rapidly and it was hard not to be scared. Finally he stood up and walked around to face her. "Don't bother to try to untie yourself. If you do you'll detonate a little surprise I've left for you or anybody who finds you while I'm gone. Each of your wrists is tied to the chair in back, just as securely as your ankles are in front. I hope you're not too uncomfortable."

Yeah, right. Bree knew that was the least of Bo's concerns. Bree had to hold back the scream building in her throat. Her panic level was growing by the instant. She tried to collect herself for a moment, feel God's presence. There had to be dozens of people praying for her by now. Surely that should give her strength. When she finally spoke, her voice was calm. "As if you really cared. All you want is those disks. Once you get them you're going to come back here and kill me anyway, aren't you, Bo?"

Bo's calm expression clouded over for the first time. "How can you suggest such a thing? I've already told you that if the disks are where you say they are and what you say they are, I'll be coming back to let you free before I leave for my new location."

"Right. Like you've told me Scooter didn't get hurt. And I seem to remember you were concerned about my fixing your computer right away because it held important records about blood donors for the drive at your company."

"A mere oversight." Bo waved a soft hand. "I couldn't tell you what those records were really about. You wouldn't understand, nor did you need to be involved."

"This could still end now, Bo," Bree told him softly. She looked into his face, searching for any caring and compassion there. There had to be some way to draw him closer, to make her count for something so he wouldn't kill her. "You wouldn't be in very much trouble. You could turn yourself in, surrender the records, and make a clean start at things. I know you've been looking for something all the time I've known you. The answer doesn't lie down the path you've traveled."

Bo gave a short bark of laughter. "You didn't really fall for that 'seeker' routine I used on you, did you, Trehearn? I knew you'd respond to a confused, lonely individual the most, so that is what I became for you. I know where I'm going, Bree. I make my own destiny. Your pathetic pretend religion has nothing to do with my life."

"Then I can't help you. But I can ask you one more time to let me go." Bree's shivering turned into trembling. She was so afraid.

"Now, you know I can't do that, Bree. And don't worry about screaming when I'm gone. We're so far out in the mangrove swamps that no one could hear you except the alligators. Save your voice for when you'll want it later." His grin as he walked out the door was positively evil.

"Remind me again how I let you talk me into this," Harry said to Cody. They were crouched behind a stand of bushes near the door of the office at Island Breeze, just close enough to see anybody going in, just far enough away to be inconspicuous.

"I didn't give you a choice. And besides, where else would you get this much free trained help?"

"Yeah, I don't like that part either." Harry's expression was somber. "Too many civilians know about this."

"I couldn't do it any other way." Anyone coming into the complex would see a party down by the pool and little or no activity by the office, which was the way he wanted it. Shawn was playing DJ with his boom box under the picnic pavilion, while Marisa and the kids passed out punch to the vacationers who just happened to be Bree's personal prayer chain. What looked like a party was in fact something else, but to anyone looking, it would appear to be a party.

"I still don't think it's such a great idea," Harry argued. "You should have let me do this my way, with a real stakeout and more officers."

Cody shook his head, then realized immediately that Harry probably couldn't see him in the dark. "Wouldn't work that way, my friend. This guy would spot it in a minute."

"And you think he won't spot us?"

"Not the two old pros we are." Cody prayed that he was right. "Besides, we're not going to do anything to let him know we're here."

"Good thing, because I think he's about to take us up on the offer," Harry said. A car with rental company plates and a lone occupant cruised by the front of the buildings. It was a nondescript sedan, and Cody was pretty sure he wouldn't have noticed it on most nights. This car could have slipped in and out of the complex before with no one the wiser.

The car pulled past once and left the front parking lot of the complex, going back out on the street. Cody and Harry kept silent, waiting to see if Bo would come back or if it had simply been a tourist looking for someplace to stay the night.

Come on. It all looks fine. Just pull back in and park. As if the driver of the silver sedan had heard him, the car nosed back into the lot and pulled into a parking space halfway between their hiding place and the office door.

Harry gave him the high sign. "Now we just wait," he whispered so low that Cody could barely hear.

The two of them waited. The driver of the car got out quietly and slipped to the door of the office. In a moment he was in, and Cody silently complimented him on his skills. Normally getting into Island Breeze that quietly without a key would've been impossible. Of course, tonight Cody had conveniently forgotten to secure the most challenging of the locks. Still, it took a little doing.

There was the gleam of a small flashlight inside. "It

should take him a couple minutes, no longer," Cody said. "I still wish we could bug the car, just in case he's a better driver than we expect or we lose him."

"We won't lose him. If we do, it will be your fault because you're driving, my friend."

Cody felt a flush of surprise. "What? I didn't think that was going to happen."

"Yeah, well, I've got cars around the island, but you are definitely the guy who's driving. We've got the radio set up on a channel most folks wouldn't think to access, and the minute we figure out where he's going, we'll have company. But I need to deal with the radio, so you need to drive. That okay with you?"

"Wouldn't have it any other way. Hand me the keys." Cody prayed silently as he held out his hand. There wasn't even a jingle as Harry slipped him the keys to a sedan even more nondescript than the rental car. "Should we get over there and hunker down?"

"Only if you're positive you can do it before he comes out of there," Harry said.

"I'm pretty sure I can, if I'm not permanently stiff from hiding behind this bush."

"Yeah, well, you could have told me your complex was infested with ants," Harry groused. "I think somebody's been having a party in my left sock for the last fifteen minutes."

"Hazards of the job." Cody shrugged. "Let's get

moving before the bad guy gets back out here."

In what felt like many long minutes but was probably more like seconds, they were both crouched in Harry's unmarked car, nearly sitting on the floorboards. Harry had an ingenious arrangement of mirrors that let them sit there and still be able to see out of the car.

"He's coming out the front, and he's coming fast." Harry slid even deeper into the shadows. "Let's hope nobody gets anywhere close to him, because he seems to have an unholstered semiautomatic in his right hand."

Cody broke out in a cold sweat. He had forgotten the rush of adrenaline that police work gave him. Part excitement, part dread, part fear, it was a mix of feelings that had been almost addictive for many years. Somehow after Dave died, he never had this same rush again. Until now. And now the rush came from the excitement that Bree needed him and they were going to find her.

They had to.

After a few agonizing moments, Harry gave him the signal to start the engine. "No lights, not for a while."

"Did you really need to tell me that?" Cody asked. "I haven't been out of the game that long."

Harry shrugged. "Better to tell and not need than

not remind you and have it be the one thing you didn't remember." They were still low in their seats when the car rolled out of the Island Breeze parking lot. Up ahead, about a block down the street that led to Periwinkle Way, was the silver rental car. It had an odd pattern on one taillight that Cody hadn't noticed before.

"You do that?" Cody motioned ahead to the back of the car. "Nice work."

"Amazing what you can do with a little sticky tree junk or mud. If you do it quickly and quietly and don't mess up the light too much, they won't notice. Nobody looks at their taillights," Harry said. "It's not as effective as a bug, but it's sure a lot easier."

They cruised down onto Periwinkle, heading toward the business district, the causeway, and Captiva. "Now which way will he go?" Cody turned to Harry. "I'm betting on Captiva, myself, or at least the end of Sanibel past the Ding Darling," he said, referring to the wild growth of nature preserve that made up nearly a third of the island.

"Looks like you're right." They followed the car past the road to the causeway, and neither of them turned. "I can't imagine anyplace else he could be going that would be so isolated that we haven't found him yet."

Harry picked up the radio and began transmitting.

He gave out the rental car's license plate and description to his cohorts around the island and described their location. "This way we can pull back a little before he ever gets suspicious."

"We can pull back, but I'm not going to stop. I'm in on this one all the way, Harry."

"That goes without saying. Just ease back a little for now. Ray and Richter are going to pull out in front of him right up there at Bailey's Plaza. He can't be expecting a tail elaborate enough to have three teams, which is what we're going to give him."

Even though it was all going according to plan, the back of Cody's neck prickled. He knew from experience his anxiety wouldn't let up until the whole mess was over, one way or another. It was almost like being back at the wheel with Dave.

There was one major difference for which Cody was thankful. This time they had a third rider in the car, and Cody was sure that the third rider was the one in charge. No matter how nervous he felt, or how scared, he was able to put Bree in God's hands tonight. Even watching the back of the silver car so intently he was ready to jump out of his skin, Cody still knew he was in God's hands himself, and that God was in control. It made police work feel vastly different. He still would be ready to give it up for good after tonight, but this way it was bearable.

He wiped each of his sweaty palms on his khakis. How far could they be going? No more than five or six miles or they'd run out of island. It was going to be the longest five or six miles of his life.

"Whoa. Hold on to your hat and gun it," Harry said suddenly. The rental car surged ahead of Ray and Richter and squealed down the road at high speed. It was turning into a chase.

"We can't lose him." Cody gritted his teeth and accelerated. "If we do, we might not find Bree." He couldn't finish the sentence all the way. His real fear was that if they lost Bowen, they wouldn't find Bree *alive*. No matter what, he didn't want that to be the outcome of their chase.

The Sanibel-Captiva road was dark and winding. It was the perfect place to lose pursuers, and Bowen was using it to his advantage. Adding to Cody's frustration, there were still other people on the road he had to look out for. "We should have found some way to do road-blocks up here," he said, bouncing hard in his seat as the car hit a hole at high speed.

"Yeah, we should have. But we didn't, so we're going to have to rely on your superior driving skills, my friend." They rounded a corner on the twisting road and Harry swore, loudly and fluently. Bowen and the silver car had vanished in the couple of seconds they'd had in front of them on the turn.

"Okay, where did he go?" Harry's eyes scanned the darkness. "Down that path into the mangroves over to the right, or up that gravel road? There's been enough rain lately he wouldn't raise dust either way."

Cody forced himself to be still for a moment, praying for guidance. "Right. Into the mangroves. Send one of the teams down the gravel, in case I'm wrong."

"And I'll have the other one follow us in there, in case you're right," Harry told him. "I have a strong hunch you're right. Down that path someplace is the building site that was going to be an Orlando Magic player's hideaway retreat, until he got traded last season. All that ever got done was part of a foundation and a construction shack. It would be the perfect place to hide out."

Cody glared at Harry. "And you didn't search it?"

"I was looking at places with more human contact. This one just came to me."

They rounded another curve in the dirt-and-gravel path and nearly ran up the back of the silver car. The driver's door was open and the engine still running, but it was empty. Cody slammed on the brakes and narrowly missed hitting the empty car. Harry poured out his side and a wave of panic washed over Cody.

"Remember, he's armed. You saw that pistol," he yelled to Harry. "Don't give him a target."

"Don't worry." Harry kept the car door open

between him and the road as a barrier. "I think he's headed for the shack anyway. It should be just over the rise."

They both left the car, moving cautiously. Cody couldn't help feeling he was in somebody's sights. What if Bowen had a confederate? They hadn't considered it because all the information they had said he worked alone. But what if he'd changed his pattern, just to lead them on?

The night noises seemed overwhelming. Cody hoped they weren't too deep into the area between the swamps and mangrove roots that they'd have company in the form of alligators. It was the last thing he needed back here.

Ahead he could see the dim glow of a light between the trees and bushes. Behind he could hear the slam of more car doors as the other patrol team pulled up. They were closing in on Bowen. Cody fought the urge to holler just to let off steam.

The showdown came in a split second. There was a flash of light glinting off metal and the spit of a semiautomatic weapon. Harry backed up and pushed Cody over, then got to his knees and fired a warning shot high in the direction of the shot that whizzed past him.

"Police, Bowen. Drop the gun and come out now," Harry called. Cody struggled to his feet, ignoring Harry's motions to stay still. Charging in a wide arc around the grassy hummock where the shack stood, Cody circled around to the door. It stood open and the interior of the place yawned dark in front of him.

Bowen might be in there with a gun, but even if he was, Cody was going after Bree. He had to go in there now. "Father, protect me. Protect us both." He dashed into the space.

The first room was dark. He could see a connecting doorway leading to someplace else. In an instinctive shooter's crouch, he surveyed the front room. Empty. He went quickly to the doorway and his heart nearly stopped.

Bree sat in a straight-backed chair. Her hands and legs seemed to be tied to the chair, and her head slumped far forward. She looked—

Cody pushed the thought away as his pulse jumped into overdrive. *God, please, don't let anything have happened to her.* "Bree," he called. It was more of a croak.

Her head came up, and a wave of relief swept over him.

"Cody!" The tears in her voice tore at his heart. "Praise God, you're here." Her pale, drawn face was such a welcome sight now that she was talking and her eyes were open. She arched her head back, shaking. "Don't come any closer. Bo said he wired the chair with explosives. If you touch me, we might both go up."

All Cody wanted to do was run to her, pick her up,

chair and all, and carry her out of this ratty building. He steeled himself to walk carefully and slowly over to the chair instead. "We'll see about that, sweetheart. Do you know what a sight for sore eyes you are, even tied to a chair?"

Bree started crying then, and Cody fought an even more powerful urge to scoop her up.

There was an exchange of gunfire near the door to the shack. Both of them looked up, heads swinging toward the noise.

"North?" Cody heard Harry call out. "We got him. Situation over. You okay in there?"

"We'll be fine. I need a lot more light," Cody yelled back. "And we may need the guys from the Fort Myers bomb squad. I'll let you know once I get the light."

He put his hand softly, gently, on top of Bree's head. "It's over." The words were meant to be reassuring, but they came out choked. Cody cleared his throat to try again. "I'll get you out of this as quickly as I can."

Bree tilted her head so Cody's hand slid down her cheek. He could feel her tears and sweat there, and then her soft lips as they brushed his palm. "I'll get you out of this. . . with God's help." He bowed his head, and as naturally as if he'd done it every day he began to pray, asking God to protect them, to keep him calm and alert.

Finished, he opened his eyes and found Bree's teary

gaze on him. "The hard part is over now, sweetheart." He gave thanks that his voice had steadied. He gave her as cocky a grin as he could muster, considering the fact that his insides felt like Jell-O. "From here on out, things are just going to get better."

Eighteen

"SO, WHAT DO YOU SEE?" BREE LOOKED DOWN AT CODY. He had a light on her chair now and had been back there quite a while. The silence was more deafening than the noise of the shoot-out had been.

"Nothing that would warrant the bomb squad coming out from Fort Myers. You're fastened to the chair with duct tape. There's a shoebox wrapped in foil under the chair, with wires leading from it to the duct tape. Can you feel something like wires poking you?"

"Yes." Bree had trouble getting the words out of her cotton-dry mouth. "I figured that was the bomb."

"That's what Bowen wanted you to think. But it seems to be a decoy. It did its job, anyway. And it's still going to keep doing its job, because I'm not so positive that it's fake that I'd risk your safety. You mean too much to me to take the chance."

"Anybody sitting in this chair would mean that much to you, Cody." Bree tried to be honest with herself as she said it. "I've seen the way you care for life in general. Dave taught you that, didn't he?"

"I guess he did," Cody said slowly. "After his passing, I knew for sure that everything was so precious. I guess I just didn't find a way to voice that belief until you came along."

Bree couldn't hold back a nervous giggle. "This is a strange conversation to be having while I'm taped to a chair. If you can't move me, could you at least get me a drink of water? I'm really, really thirsty."

"Sure. I'll be right back." It set her heart racing to watch him walk to the doorway.

"Don't leave!" He spun around, and Bree felt her face flame at the panic that had just coursed through her. "I want the water, but I don't think I can be alone again."

"Sure, sweetheart." He stood in the doorway and called to someone on the other side. "Harry? The lady would like a drink of water. Can you hand me in something?" He waited a minute at the doorway, and Bree saw someone give him a cylindrical bottle.

They exchanged a few words that Bree couldn't make out, and Cody nodded. "Okay, thanks."

"Bo? Is he in custody?" Bree asked.

"He is. Some of that noise we heard a few minutes ago was an ambulance taking him to Fort Myers. He and Ray were both wounded in the crossfire."

"I'm not glad he's hurt." Bree blinked back tears. "But I *am* glad he's not dangerous anymore."

"We all are." Cody opened the cap on the bottle of water, and held it to her mouth. "I know this is going to be awkward, but until we get somebody that knows more than I do to look at this box, I can't chance moving you."

"I understand." She took a drink from the bottle. It felt cool and wonderful, even though part of it dribbled down her chin. Actually, that felt almost as good as drinking it.

"Is it still the fifth?" Bree asked. "I've lost track of time."

"I believe it's actually early on the sixth. I haven't looked at a watch in a while myself. You had us too busy to do that, Miss Bree. And while I've got you here as a captive audience, explain to me how you thought the inside of your computer case was a safe place for those files."

"It seemed like a good idea when I did it." She shook her head. "Now nothing I've done in the last ten weeks or so sounds like a good idea. I've messed up so many lives, including my own. Are the kids okay?"

"Everyone is fine. You're the one the worst for

wear, Bree." Cody stroked her face, his gaze softening. "I know the moment we get you out of that chair you're going to want to go home and take a long shower."

"And eat something, and burn these clothes," Bree agreed. "And then sleep for about two days. That is, if your friends in the next room will let me."

"I'll make sure they leave you alone as long as I can. At least for a few hours to get you back to somewhat near normal. It's different being on the outside of things in an investigation like this. I'm seeing everything from such a different perspective."

"Do you like this view?" She wondered if being in action for a few hours would draw him back to police work.

"It's just fine. It makes digging out bushes at the complex look very, very good." Cody's eyes were somber. "If I never do this again, it will be okay with me."

Bree felt a surge of relief almost equal to what she'd felt when Cody came through the door. "Good. I don't want to have to worry about you. Which I would do if you went back to police work. I couldn't stop you or anything, but I sure wouldn't like it."

Cody arched one eyebrow. "Oh, so you're staying around now?"

"If you'll let me," Bree told him. "The last two days have told me where I need to be, Cody. My new home is here on Sanibel Island. I think it's here on the island with you, but that part is in God's hands. I know now he didn't really lead me down here. At least not for the reasons I thought he did."

"No, he probably didn't. But I think you're right about one thing. While you were off on your squirrel hunt, he steered you to me." Cody knelt by her side and made her drink another sip of the water. Bree wasn't sure if he was giving her a drink to take care of her or to give himself more time to put his words together.

His eyes glowed with a golden light. "You have driven me nuts, Bree Trehearn. You've done everything you weren't supposed to and turned my world upside down. But in the same moments you were driving me crazy, you were also giving me this gigantic push into the arms of Jesus. Nobody else could have pushed me like that, lady. I owe you my life in a far different way than you think you owe me yours."

Bree was crying again. She could feel the tears course down her face. "Maybe that makes all this worth it, Cody." He reached up and gently smoothed away her tears.

She had to laugh when he grimaced. "Now what's the matter?"

"My hands are dirty. Stop crying, Bree, you're getting your face even more streaked than it was before and I can't fix it. For somebody who doesn't wear mascara you sure have some huge black stripes running down your face. The news cameras at the hospital are going to get lovely photos of you."

Bree jerked her head up. "News cameras? And what is this about a hospital? I am not going to any hospital. I thought you said I could have some time to put myself together."

"I said I'd keep the cops away from you for as long as possible, sweetheart. I didn't say where I'd be able to do that. I'm experienced enough to know that you'll be going to the hospital to be checked out, whether you like it or not," he told her. "So don't argue anymore. And don't pull on those wires. I have been wrong before, you know."

"Yes, sir." For now she'd sit still and stop arguing. She would treasure the sight of Cody kneeling beside her and be happy in the moment. But once they got her loose from this chair, things were going to be a different story. She hadn't lost all her stubbornness in the last day and a half.

They ended up waiting for the Fort Myers bomb squad guys anyway. Harry didn't want the responsibility of dismantling the device any more than Cody did. Even after the team that came pronounced the device harmless and removed the shoebox, Bree sweated through their slitting the tape and removing wires. It felt so good to move her arms and legs again once she was free.

She didn't have any luck protesting a trip to the hospital, either. Just as Cody said, they insisted that she go. She felt silly being loaded onto a stretcher and put in an ambulance. There was nothing wrong with her that a shower and a good night's sleep wouldn't cure. However, nobody would take her word for that.

Cody wanted to stay with her the whole time. He got pretty hot under the collar when the emergency medical technicians wouldn't let him on the ambulance. "Sorry, sir," the one woman on the crew told him. She was the one standing up to him, even though she was probably all of five-feet-two and weighed about a hundred pounds with full gear on. "The lady needs a police escort and that's who's going to be riding with her. You're not family, you're not police."

"Yes, but I promised her I wouldn't leave her." Cody had a gleam in his eye that made Bree wonder if he was going to get himself in trouble. He looked like he was ready to make an end run around the EMT and get on the ambulance whether they wanted him to or not.

Instead he turned and bellowed Harry's name. The big police detective was at his side in a minute. "What now?" Harry looked tired to Bree. She was so grateful for him and the rest of the police officers who'd spent a large portion of the last day looking for her. She kept sending up prayers for the one who got hurt. Was his name Ray? If it wasn't, she knew God knew who she was praying for.

Harry and Cody were arguing about his riding in the ambulance. Finally Harry threw up his hands and turned to the EMT. "Go ahead. Let him on instead of one of my guys. I know it's not policy, but we haven't done anything according to policy since Cody inserted himself into this investigation. Might as well finish up the way we started. He'll be as responsible as anybody from my unit and probably guard her even better."

Bree drifted in and out of sleep on the ambulance ride. It was cool and pleasant, even with the vehicle moving at high speed. Cody held her hand, looking down at her intently. "I need to tell you so many things, Bree." There were lines etched in his tanned face that Bree didn't remember from before. It hurt to think that worry over her might have put them there.

"It might have to wait, Cody." She was conscious of the fact that her own voice seemed to come from far, far away. "I'm not holding on too well right now. In fact, I think I'm beginning to see why Harry thought this trip was a good idea." Things were fuzzy for a while after that.

She remembered the transfer into the hospital. There seemed to be a lot of emergency vehicles and police cars there. Bree wondered at the number of uniformed officers she saw but didn't have the stamina to wonder long. She got the idea that something was going on, something more than her arrival. Of course, she remembered that the wounded officer had been taken here. Maybe all this ruckus was standard procedure when you had a police officer shot.

One of Harry's men joined them while they were waiting in the bay of the emergency room. Again, Cody never left her side. Even when the nurse gave him a pointed look and told him straight out that they were going to undress the patient and he'd have to step outside, Cody stood his ground. Bree didn't know Cody could blush like that. "Is she the one..." the nurse started to ask while Cody argued that he wasn't going outside and neither was the Sanibel officer.

"She's the one. And we're not saying any more." Cody flashed her a pointed look that silenced the nurse. Bree thought that was a pretty neat trick. She didn't look like the kind of person easily silenced. He and the officer turned their backs while Bree slipped out of her clothes and into a hospital gown, but neither of them left. Cody didn't even let go of her hand, still holding his body turned away from her, until she had to deal with the sleeve and strap on that arm.

She wondered what the nurse had been going to ask, but her treating the abrasions left by the duct tape on Bree's ankle distracted her from any questions of her own. It was just too painful a process to focus on a train of thought.

The only time Bree had ever had drugs to put her
to sleep was when she had her wisdom teeth out at fifteen. Still, she would almost have sworn that something similar had been slipped into her water bottle
sometime during the rescue. Why else was she so
foggy? The nurses and doctors assured her that exhaus-
tion and stress could do that to a person. Bree had to
struggle to answer their questions in a clear manner.

They moved her to a bed on a medical floor for
observation for a few hours. Bree thought that was silly.
She knew that all anybody was going to be observing of
her was deep sleep. A sweet young nursing student
stayed in the bathroom and talked to her while she took
a quick shower. She expected it was to make sure that
she didn't fall asleep standing up and drown. Outside in
the bedroom she could hear Cody and the same young
Sanibel police officer talking about something. They
stopped when she came back into the room dressed
after her shower.

It felt so good to be in a clean bed, with cool, crisp
sheets around her. Even the double set of hospital
gowns she was wearing instead of pajamas didn't bother
her. The one worn backward over the first one cut out
the annoying gaps, and they were both soft and clean.
Cody didn't even laugh at her outfit. He seemed pre-
occupied by something, but Bree couldn't figure out
what.

He was still there when she went to sleep, kissing her softly on the forehead. At first Bree didn't think she could possibly sleep in a hospital room, surrounded by the sounds and smells of the institution. And there was so much noise. How did anybody sleep through that? But her head had barely hit the pillow before she was gone.

Waking up felt like a scene from *The Wizard of Oz*. Firmly etched in Bree's memory from childhood was that scene at the end of the classic movie where Dorothy wakes up in her own bed and she's surrounded by everybody but Miss Gulch. When she awoke, light streamed into the window of her room between the slats of the vertical blinds.

Cody sat by her bedside, talking softly but intently to Harry. Shawn sat in the other chair across the bed. "Hey, Dad. I think she's awake," were the first words Bree heard clearly enough to decipher.

"She is. Sort of," Bree said. It felt as if an army of carpenter ants had built something in her mouth while she slept. "What day is it? How long did I sleep?"

"Still the sixth. You slept only a few hours. Harry seems to think you'll be alert enough to talk to soon, but I'm holding out for tomorrow."

Bree pushed herself into a sitting position. "You're sweet, but Harry's probably right. Let me get something to eat first and brush my teeth. And maybe even put my own clothes on. I'll bet Shawn brought me some clothes, didn't you?"

Shawn nodded. "Charlotte came over and picked them out. I didn't have a clue about some of the stuff. I didn't even want to know, really. She put everything in a grocery sack. I hope it's okay."

"If Charlotte helped pick it out, it will all be okay." Bree hoped Charlotte had put all kinds of goodies in that sack that Shawn or any other man might not have thought about, like lip gloss and her hairbrush and other little sundries. "So what's for breakfast around here? Or is it dinnertime already?" She couldn't judge the angle of the sun coming in the window.

Harry stepped up to the bed. He gave her a funny look, then answered her. "You're not on a restricted diet. You can have whatever you want for breakfast. I'll go anyplace you want and get it for you, especially if you talk to me."

"You're just trying a bribe," Cody growled. "And don't tell me you're not, because I haven't forgotten that much about being on the force. Leave her alone, Harry, and I'll go get her breakfast."

Bree held up a hand, trying to keep it from shaking. She wasn't feeling nearly as strong yet as she thought. "Down, boys. Harry can get me breakfast. I don't think I'm ready for you to leave yet, Cody. I'd like pancakes and bacon. Three slices of very crisp bacon and plenty of syrup for the pancakes. And a big glass of orange juice, with ice in it."

"Yes, ma'am." Harry grinned. Smiling made the skin around his eyes crinkle up. He didn't look quite so worn out that way.

"Cody, if you want to help me here, find out how long they have to keep me. I'd really like to get out of here and go back home. That is, if you'll have me."

"Oh, I'll have you, Bree." His golden eyes flashed fire when he smiled. "There are three kids back there at Island Breeze who would never let me forget it if I didn't have you back, and pronto. I think Sarita and Gabe would have hitchhiked to the hospital if they could have this morning."

"When I left they were sitting out on the front stoop on Jacaranda," Shawn told her. "Sarita had her arms around Gabe, and they were both watching the entrance to the complex. I don't think they're moving until Dad's truck comes back with you in it."

"Then I'd better shoo you all out of here and get dressed." Bree reached for the bag with her stuff in it. "That way once Harry comes back with my pancakes and we have our little chat, I can go home. Right, Harry?" She tried to bat her eyes at him, but she knew she was no good at flirtation.

"I'll do what I can, Ms. Trehearn," Harry told her. "Let me get started on finding that breakfast. And I'll try to hunt up the attending physician to make sure you're ready to release." He turned back at the door, looking over his shoulder at her. "Of course, we still need statements from you. Especially now that—"

Cody stood next to her, cutting off Harry's words with his movement. "Let's deal with that later, okay?" Bree wondered what they were keeping from her. Whatever it was, she wasn't going to worry about it, she decided, leaning back against the stack of pillows. God was in control and she was going to rest in that fact. So far everything had been provided at the right moment when she surrendered her trust to him. That wasn't going to change now.

Nineteen

WHY WERE THEY ALL WATCHING HER EAT? BREE SAT ON the edge of the bed, finishing what she could of her pancakes. It was hard to eat anything with everybody watching her. Harry and Cody seemed to be arguing without saying a word. Even Shawn seemed tense.

Finally he was the one who stood up. "I don't think this is fair, Dad. She has to know sometime. Don't you think she's going to turn on the radio or television soon? I mean, when I went to get the ice, I could hear the report on TV from every room down the hall."

A spasm of irritation crossed Cody's face. "Shawn, that's enough." Shawn stopped, still looking mutinous. It was his look, added to everything else, that told Bree something far more serious than she had imagined was going on.

Bree put down her fork. She'd definitely had enough pancakes. "Tell me what, Cody? Remember that you're talking to the lady who doesn't lie to little kids. I'd like the same courtesy. Something happened since I got to the hospital, didn't it?"

Harry and Cody looked at each other and seemed to come to a decision. "Bowen is dead, Ms. Trehearn," Harry said. "He bled to death in a stairwell of the hospital."

Bree stared at him, struggling to take in what he'd said. Bo? Dead? "That doesn't make sense. I thought you said he was just being treated for a minor gunshot wound. How did he bleed to death, and in a stairwell?"

"He wasn't hurt that badly." Harry leaned forward in his chair next to the bed. "This hospital is the only level-one trauma center in the area, so he and Ray were both rushed here. Ray's wound was more serious, and there was quite a bit of commotion while he was being treated. Even though Bowen was strapped to a gurney, he somehow managed to slip off."

"They think he was waiting for you, Bree," Cody said. "The minute the hospital saw he was missing, they closed down the hospital and the grounds, and we threw up a police barricade. They found him about four this morning in a stairwell. Apparently he'd tried to hide long enough to get to you when you came in."

"The nurses admitted later that someone might

286

have said something about you coming into the same emergency room. It was soon after that he slipped out of custody," Harry continued. "He was determined to still do some damage. He just didn't realize he was wounded badly enough that he slowly bled to death while he waited."

Bree leaned back in her chair, suddenly so weary she could hardly think straight. "So is that why you haven't left me?" She looked at Cody. "You were still protecting me from Bo?"

"It was part of why I didn't leave." He didn't look directly into her eyes. Bree's head was starting to spin. She lifted her legs back up on the bed and leaned against the pillows. This was hard to come to terms with.

"At least now I see what you mean about my talking to you being important. There isn't any other way to decipher those disks, is there?"

"Not unless they find the computer expert Bowen nearly blew up. That college kid, Scooter Harris. But he seems to have gone into hiding."

Cody glared at Harry again for letting out more information. Bree felt as if she were being protected by a tiger. Cody seemed determined to keep all harm and bad news away from her, whether she wanted things that way or not.

"You don't think he's dead too, do you?" she asked.

"Who, Harris? No, we know he's alive. Bowen blew up his car about five days ago, probably as a warning. But Harris was seen after that. We know he's alive—just in hiding."

That relieved Bree. It was hard to think of how many lives were touched by her dumb decisions. And now one of those people touched had paid the ultimate price. "Poor Bo." She sighed. It made her shiver to think about him, so filled with hate and violence even at the end. What could it possibly be like to die so alone and full of fear and anger? Bree was sickened at the thought.

Hearing all this made up Bree's mind. She had things to do that couldn't wait. "I need to go to the station to talk to Harry," she said, sitting up.

"That can still wait. I want you to come back to the complex and rest." Cody's anger made his voice sharp.

"It can't wait." Bree tilted her head back and grabbed his wrist. The tendons there were taut as piano wire, but she was determined to prove her point. "I have to do what I should have done in the first place, Cody. And now is the time to do it. If I hadn't waited this long, maybe Bo wouldn't be dead."

"Maybe." Cody shrugged. "He looked like a bomb waiting to self-destruct to me. Don't blame yourself for anything that happened to him, Bree."

"I know. But I can blame myself for all the things that happened, or nearly happened, to all of you because of him. And it's still important to set as many things right as possible."

She turned to Harry. "Are they ready to dismiss me? If not, can I sign out without consent? I want to get this over with. Then I have to get back to Island Breeze so I can finish packing."

Cody looked as if he'd been punched in the face. "I thought we settled that. I thought you were staying."

Bree shook her head. "Circumstances were different then. Knowing what I know now puts things in a different light, Cody."

He stood beside the bed, challenging her. "You can't be serious. You can't possibly leave now."

"I can, and I will," Bree said through tense lips. "Now if you'll excuse me, I have to go make a statement."

This couldn't be happening. Cody knew he hadn't done everything he'd done in the last twenty-four hours just to lose Bree. Surely this couldn't be God's will for them. But how could he make the stubborn woman he had grown to love see his point of view?

Getting her to see things his way by talking to her hadn't worked so far. She had insisted on being left at the Sanibel police station with Harry once they'd released her from the hospital. How could one beautiful young woman contain that much stubbornness? Cody fumed trying to come up with an answer to his problem.

He couldn't let Bree come home just to leave. Island Breeze was her home now. It was where she belonged. It was where God wanted her. Cody was sure of both things. There had to be a way to make Bree see that she was needed here, belonged here. She wouldn't believe it if he simply told her.

"God, you can't let her leave. I need her. I love her."

Tell her that. Show her that. The answer was clear. It sounded unbelievably simple to Cody, too simple. But then since Bree had come into his life and brought him back, face-to-face with God, things had been very simple. That simplicity was what he'd missed for so long when he turned his back on the Lord. It was Bree's childlike faith that made ripples of love around her that spread in an ever-widening pool that included him, the Montoyas, everybody around her. It was that simplicity stated again and again in so many ways that had given Cody his newfound peace.

Now God seemed to be telling him that all he had to do to get Bree to stay was reflect that simplicity and love back at her. It was worth a try. Cody didn't know how he could pull things off, but he would give it a shot. If this was what God wanted him to do to keep Bree here, things would all work out.

This is going to be hard. Bree steeled herself to do what she had to do as the police car rounded the final turn before the Island Breeze driveway. She didn't want to leave, but it was for the best. She'd messed up everyone's lives with her mad dash to Florida, and it was time to undo everything while she still could.

She could undo most of it, anyway. Her own life would never be the same. She'd always carry a deep love for Cody North. But she couldn't stay here and make that love grow. It wouldn't be fair to Cody after all the things that had happened. And it wouldn't be fair to herself to stay, knowing that he was more worried about her than in love with her.

If he'd actually professed love at some point, or any other feelings than worry and maybe gratitude, she could think of staying. But even if Cody told her that he loved her, staying would be hard now, when she felt so strongly that she bore the burden of another person's death. Ever since Harry told her about Bo, she had mental images of him slipping away like a wounded animal into the stairwell. He had lived alone and died alone, and the image haunted Bree.

This whole flight to Florida looked like such a bad

idea now. If she had stayed in Indiana, perhaps she could have gone to the police there and Bo would be in custody, alive. He could turn his life around and maybe even find Jesus through someone else in prison. Instead it was now too late for him...forever.

Scooter was hiding out somewhere, too scared to come out and face the world. Marisa Montoya was off work with three small children to support, her leg broken because of a comedy of errors Bree had too big a part in to feel secure. Where would the list of recriminations end?

They were at the parking lot of the complex now. Harry had insisted on driving her back himself. "Are you ready to do this, Bree? And are you truly sure it's the right thing for you to do?"

"No, I'm not ready, and I'm not sure anymore. Keep driving up to the lighthouse, okay, Harry?"

"Sure." Harry followed the winding road through the park and up to the lighthouse on the point. Almost every picture of Sanibel Island had this lighthouse in it. Old and worn, it still provided a beacon.

Bree got out of the car and walked up to the lighthouse. "Show me your way, Lord. Make it as clear as this lighthouse. Help me to see your light and leading on my path."

She stood in the sand looking up at the sturdy metal-and-wooden structure, covered in rust but still

standing. Watching the gulls circle, hearing their raucous cries in the sharp salt air, Bree took in the lighthouse. God was so much like that lighthouse. He never
moved, was always there and constant. All she had to
do was keep her focus there, on the Light.

She could hear Harry walking up behind her. "Do
you need some more time?"

"No, I think I'm ready to go face the music now."
Bree turned to talk to him. Her back was to the lighthouse now, but she saw a marvelous thing. The shadow
of the tall tower fell over her and Harry. Even looking
away, the lighthouse was still there. The sight strength-
ened her resolve to stop coming up with her own
answers. Whatever was waiting for her at Island Breeze,
God was in control.

"Looks like you've got a little welcoming commit-
tee," Harry said a few moments later when they pulled
into the parking lot of the complex.

The last of Bree's wavering resolve to leave faded
when the car stopped and she looked out at the scene
in front of her.

"What's that kid wearing on her head?" Harry
asked.

"I have absolutely no idea." It looked like a home-
made party hat, partially decorated with palm fronds.

"You got an answer for my second question?"
Harry asked as they got out of the car.

293

"Not if it's how they got that hat on Gabriel." Her downcast mood of the whole day was dissolving into giggles. Gabe did not look happy in his party hat. But then Bree suspected that Gabe would not have looked happy in any article of human clothing, most especially a party hat.

Sarita bounced down the walk, arms flung wide. "Bree! You're back!" She threw her arms around Bree's legs, nearly knocking them both over.

"I'm back." Bree picked up the sweet child for a hug. Having a laughing Sarita in her arms felt good. It was one of the things she'd looked forward to, promised herself would happen again when she was in the horrible room next to Bo. "Where'd you get the cool hat?"

Sarita giggled, patting her headgear. "Mr. Cody helped us make them. He's got one too, only no flowers."

"You have to draw the line somewhere," a deep voice said from the doorway. "Come on in before everybody's ice melts, Bree."

She put Sarita down to go into the building and picked Gabe up. He had gotten rid of the hat and seemed much happier without it. "Poor skinny kitty." She held him while he purred like a motorboat. "You stopped eating, didn't you?"

"He missed you something fierce." Something in

Cody's voice caught her attention. She looked at him, and the expression on his face made her pulse jump. "In all the commotion at the hospital, I don't think I said how much I missed you, either."

Bree buried her face in the cat's fur, trying to compose herself. Gabe's cool nose was moist on her cheek, and his whiskers tickled. "Are you really having a party in here?"

"We are." Cody took her arm and drew her gently into the room. "I couldn't think of a better way to show you how much you're needed here than rallying the troops. Come on in, Bree."

She let herself be led into her apartment, where a chair sat in the middle of the room filled with cushions, like a throne. Cody guided her there and made her sit down. The little apartment was full of people.

Charlotte and Ed came up to her first. Bree noticed that Charlotte wore one of the hats. Hers was appropriately trimmed with hot pink streamers. "You can't just pick up and leave, Bree." Ed patted her shoulder. "You make too great a contribution to Island Community Church. You get everybody all fired up with your enthusiasm wherever you are. We need that here."

"Besides," Charlotte piped up, "you haven't finished getting the office modernized here yet. If you leave now, Cody will make me go back to keeping the records on stone tablets."

"I heard that," Cody growled in mock anger. "That's not the kind of thing that will convince her to stay, Charlotte."

"Give me a try then, Dad." Shawn walked up to her chair. He wore oversized shorts and an oversized party hat to match. "First of all, I want to say that my dad made me wear this hat, but he didn't make me come here to talk to you." His expressive young face spoke volumes before he even opened his mouth. "You can't go, Bree. Who's going to get me through my senior year if you're not here? Nobody else has the same kind of wild discussions with me you do.... That's all." Shawn suddenly grew shy and stepped back.

"Mama got a new cast for your party," Sarita said loudly. Bree looked around and saw it was true. Marisa sported a shorter cast and crutches.

"I still need help, Bree." Marisa's dark eyes were filled with a warm affection. "And encouragement. See, I learn that word in English just so I could say it to you." Marisa's smile was breathtaking, and Bree couldn't say anything for the emotions crowding her thoughts.

"All right. Stop already." Bree fought the lump in her throat. "So nobody wants me to leave, unless Cody does. I still think it would be for the best if I went back to Indiana. I've just messed up everybody's lives here."

Cody was beside her in a moment. "That's not

true. And nobody wants you to leave, least of all me. I want to tell you in front of everybody here that I love you, Bree."

The words washed over her, filling her with a joy she couldn't have imagined. *He loves me!* Quick tears filled her eyes. *Oh, Father, he loves me!*

Cody's expression grew even more tender as he watched the tears slide down her face. He reached out a gentle hand to caress her face. "You came into my life with a bang and brought such a renewal with you that I can't express it. Losing you now——" his voice caught, and when he continued, the words came out low and rough—"would be like blowing out the light of my life."

"Cody…"

He pressed a finger softly to her lips, then leaned down and kissed her on the cheek. With a slow smile he slowly cupped her face, then brought his lips to hers for a sweet, long, and utterly satisfying kiss.

When he lifted his head, Bree became aware of the cheering around them. She smiled, feeling the warmth fill her cheeks.

"Bree, please say you'll stay. And then…"

She met his gaze. "Then?"

"Bree, tell me the one thing that will make my life complete."

"The——the one thing?" She could hardly breathe.

A grin split Cody's face. "Please, say I can take off this stupid hat."

It was still Cody. Bree laughed through tears. "I'll stay. And you can take off the hat. And for heaven's sake, don't put one back on Gabe. I love you, Cody. I never would have thought you could bring yourself to do something like this just to keep me." She swept a hand around the room, taking in all the people she loved, wearing goofy hats and having a party for no reason.

It looked like something she'd dream up. Not at all like something the staid, serious Cody North she'd met on the beach would invent, not in his wildest dreams.

"Oh, trust me, I didn't do it alone," Cody said, kissing her again, this time to applause. "I had plenty of help. Some of it even came from human hands." He looked down at her, serious again. "So you'll really stay?"

"I'll really stay." She ran her palm along his jaw. "You need me and you love me. That's what I needed to hear."

"Does this mean I get to plan a wedding?" Charlotte's grin went ear to ear. "I've always wanted to plan a wedding."

Bree shook her head. "Not yet, Charlotte. I know you'll be amazed to hear me, the queen of spontaneity, say this, but things like this we're going to leave in God's hands from now on."

"And that's where they belong." Cody folded his strong hands around hers as he knelt beside her. "Just like we belong together. I'm sure of it, Bree." This time his kiss was filled with the promise she saw in his golden eyes. A promise that said they would welcome each day from God and face it together, with love.

Bree's heart sang as Cody kissed her, and she nestled against him, more content than she'd ever been in her life. She'd never need to run away again. She'd found the place where she belonged, and it was beside this man, held in his arms.

At long last, she was truly home.

Dear Friends in Christ,

Sometimes things happen during the course of writing a book that change what you're writing to a vast degree. Things definitely happened that way during the writing of *Island Breeze*.

I have wanted to set a book on Sanibel Island for years. Its one of my favorite spots on earth, a real place of renewal for me. During my last trip there we celebrated my father's seventieth birthday, a marvelous gift our entire family of three generations was able to share.

Shortly after I started writing this book, my family had to deal with the unexpected death of someone close. Going through those questions we often ask at such times made me change some of the focus of the book, especially the questions Cody was asking himself.

I pray that God gives you the peace of his presence, the answer to all questions.

Yours in Christ,

Lynn Bulock

Write to Lynn Bulock c/o Palisades, P.O. Box 1720, Sisters, OR 97759

Don't miss the other exciting spring Palisades releases...

HI, HONEY, I'M HOME by Linda Windsor
ISBN: 1-57673-556-7
Available now!

Friday night traffic on the beltway was typical, but
nonetheless horrendous, particularly if one had a dead-
line. Kathryn Sinclair did. A glance at the clock on the
dash told her she had exactly one hour to deliver her
prodigal son to her neighbor's home. Then she had to
make like the devil for her own, where her assistant
manager was putting the final touches on their promo-
tional brain child—an intimate open house to display
the Emporium's latest imports. At seven o'clock, not
only would her choice customers fill the spacious living
room of her historic Georgian manor, but her employers would be there as well.

One dilemma at a time, Kathryn decided with a
sidelong glance at her small companion. Despite herself, she couldn't help drumming her manicured fingers on the steering wheel and inadvertently rocking
forward, as if that would speed up the long line of red
brake lights moving at a snail's pace ahead of her. Beside
her, eight-year-old Jason Egan stared at the menagerie
of cars, trucks, and sport utility vehicles as though the
red glow had lured him into some sort of trance.

Kathryn thought he was shaken by the parent-
teacher conference, which was making his mother late

for her business engagement. At least, she *hoped* he was! It was hard to tell. Jason was like his late father in that respect. He tacked off to more neutral ground rather than dwell on a troublesome matter. Drawing him back to the subject at hand required vise grips. She shoved a thick lock of dark hair behind her ear, checked the side mirror, and pulled over to the right lane, where traffic was coming to a stop.

"There will be no television this weekend. I expect you to make up all the homework you excused yourself from."

The computer-generated note, allegedly from her to his teacher, was a gem. He hadn't even used the spell checker!

"You already said that, Mom." Jason also possessed his late father's uncanny knack for undermining her momentum, which was amazing considering he'd spent a scant three years with the man. Most of the time Nick Egan had been a TV shot for thirty seconds here and there, hardly the real father a little boy needed and certainly not the husband she herself had hoped for when she'd fallen head over heels in love with him. She married Nick, but Nick married his job.

Kathryn mentally shook herself, refusing to be drawn back into the past when her future was about to become stalled on I-95. She resisted the urge to blow her horn as others were doing. It accomplished nothing, except to irritate those about her all the more. With her luck, some nut would break out a pistol and start taking potshots at them.

She stepped up the speed of the automatic delayed wipers instead. The wet snow that splashed on the windshield was coming down faster now, as if it hadn't made up its mind whether to make a liar out of the forecasters or not. Scattered showers was the prediction, not snow and freezing rain. But the roads were clear so far, Kathryn noted, hoping the bad turn in the weather wouldn't cut down on attendance. Last year's first show had been such a success.

"I did know all the material, Mom. Even Mrs. Himes said that," Jason reminded her, taking a stab at his defense. No afternoon cartoons was a serious penalty.

"Jason, you have to follow certain accepted rules." Kathryn held back the *unlike your father* that flashed through her mind and remained on the subject at hand. "Even if you know the work, you *must* do your home-work!"

"Maybe if I had a reason to do it," the boy began, cutting cinnamon-hued eyes at her from beneath a forelock of sandy brown hair. It was the same color Nick's had been in his boyhood pictures, before it turned darker with maturity.

It was also shaggy again and needed cutting,

although when she'd find the time for a trip to the salon was another story. From Thanksgiving to Christmas was the store's busiest time of year. She reached over and brushed the boy's bangs back, only to have them stubbornly resume their comfortable sprawl. Jason was so like Nick, even down to the long dark lashes that set off his eyes in a way a woman would die for. They had a lazy, pensive look at the moment, one Kathryn recognized from the past as well.

She felt a familiar anguish tear at her chest as she looked away from the mirror image of her late husband. Although their divorce had almost been final when Nick was killed in a terrorist explosion in some third-world city she couldn't pronounce, she hadn't been prepared for the grief that overtook her. After all, she'd been about to have him legally removed from her life.

At least that's the way it had appeared. Actually, she'd prayed that asking for a divorce would shake Nick up enough to make him realize how he was neglecting her and Jason. Good as her intention was, it backfired. When he agreed to it without a fight, she'd been so hurt and angered that she let it coast on its own momentum, against heart and reason.

Then he was taken from her forever. Nick's sudden death only drove home that there was a part of her that would always love Nick. He was her first, her only love, and God took him or allowed him to die, maybe in punishment for her foolish attempt to get her husband's attention. She swallowed back the sudden rise of bitterness from the past.

Somewhere she'd read that the human memory tended to erase the bad memories and highlight the good. While she'd contest the first part, the last she found to be true. Sometimes, when she was tired and off guard, a glance at Jason could wring the sweet images from the past and leave her undone.

Tonight she could not afford that regression. Nick always invaded her thoughts more at Christmas. She'd married him and said her final good-bye to him three years later, both on Christmas Eve. With the same resolve with which she'd reassembled her life, borne Nick the second son he never knew about, and established herself as one of the lead import buyers on the east coast, Kathryn willed the gnawing ache away. She never wanted her son to know the anguish he innocently brought her with his resemblance to his father.

"I can think of a reason to do all that work," Jason spoke up, bringing Kathryn back to the conversation at hand. He didn't look at her. Instead he concentrated on brushing away the crumbs of a snack he'd devoured while Kathryn met with his teacher.

He obviously was up to something, but that sudden emotional blast from the past dulled her ability to discern just what it was. She remained cautiously silent, wishing she had a windshield wiper for her brain.

"Soccer," the boy informed her when she glanced at him expectantly.

"I should have known." Jason also had Nick's tenacity, the ability to go after what he wanted if it took days, even weeks, until she either gave in from exasperation or forgot her initial objection. It had made his father one of the top network reporters. He always got his story.

"I'm a tough kid, Mom, and soccer's not as rough as football. I won't get hurt like Grandma says."

"You're too little! And what if you break your fingers? How will you play the piano?" Jason was a gifted musician, according to Madame Tremaine.

"I won't break my fingers! We're not allowed to touch the ball!" the child responded in grating condescension at her ignorance of the sport. "Dad was a football captain. He could have gone pro! I want to be like him, but I'll settle for soccer. Too late for football anyway."

Double wham! If Jason were any more like his father, she'd not be able to bear it. He had a sturdy build for an eight-year-old and could hold his ground like a rock according to Jim Anderson, their neighbor and pony league coach. Then there were those dark brown eyes with volatile flecks of gold that could flash with anger or dance with mischief. They'd drive some girl crazy someday.

"Jason, you know I can't take you to and from soccer practice this time of year. My time is limited even more by business." If only she weren't so worn out from getting ready for the show, she'd be quicker on her feet. As it was, Nick—no, Jason, she amended—had the advantage. "We'll discuss this later, okay?"

Kathryn would have closed her eyes in despair were the thinning cars ahead not approaching her turn.

"An' what am I going to do while the guys watch TV tonight?" Jason lamented, switching tactics smoothly. "I can't even go to my *own* room in my *own* house because of that dumb old party."

Why had she ever told the boys the house was really theirs, held in trust from their late father's estate? Dr. Spock never had a chapter on this situation. "But I am in charge of the house until you and Jeremy are twenty-one. Then you can kick me out and do what you will with it!"

Her knuckles whitened from her grasp on the steering wheel as she turned onto a county road boasting several swanky developments. Since Jason had gone into the third grade, he'd become more and more disagreeable and difficult to handle. He was learning exactly where her strings were and which ones to pull.

"In the meantime—" She broke off upon feeling her son's small hand close about her arm.

"I'd *never* kick you out, Mom. You know that."

The stricken look on Jason's face tugged at her heart. She could feel it melting beneath the contrition of his gaze.

Kathryn wanted to let go of the wheel and draw him into her arms. Instead, she shot into the right lane and passed a service van loaded with workmen. They'd obviously started their weekend celebration early, judging from the way they swerved over the line.

Her destination was just ahead. The name Brighton Heath was outlined in colonial blue and gold against a wood-planked background and illuminated by soft spotlights. Small white Christmas lights adorned the impeccably manicured plantings in the median dividing the entrance and exit to one of the metro area's more elite subdivisions.

"I know, Jason." She reached out to squeeze the boy's hand as she passed off-shooting streets marked with plaques bearing old English names of the same design as the entrance. "And you do have a point. A lot of the books you need to finish your homework are in your room."

"Does that mean I can play with the guys and watch TV?"

"Only if you give me your solemn promise to spend the rest of your weekend at home working on your catch-up work," Kathryn conceded. "Can you do that?"

She drew her free hand back to the wheel to turn into Meadow Green. As she did so, she gently tested the brakes. The car didn't lose traction, which meant that, so far, the wet snow wasn't sticking or freezing.

"Cool!" Jason's smile was back in place.

The Andersons' two-story home, designed in a French style, was aglow with Christmas candles in each window and beribboned swags of evergreen on the sills. As Kathryn maneuvered into the driveway, Karrie Anderson, clad in her typical battle-of-the-bulge regalia—a sweat suit, sweatband, and running shoes—opened the wreathed front door and waved, a steaming cup in hand.

"New tea! Guaranteed to take off pounds! Not bad either!"

"As if you need it!" Kathryn teased through the open electric window of the car. Despite a slim figure, her neighbor was always on some diet or exercise kick.

With the Andersons' two boys of six and eight, she supposed it was too much to hope that her younger son, Jeremy, would poke his little face through the open door to greet her. Jason, however, did deign to give her a hasty peck on the cheek.

"Thanks, Mom! Hope you have a good party!" Bundled in a down-filled jacket, he practically rolled out the car door and dashed for the house.

"Good luck tonight!" Karrie called out to her,

backing against the glass storm door to let Jason barrel past.

"Thanks! And thanks for keeping the boys. I'll pick them up as soon as the trucks take the goods back to the store!"

Karrie's cheerful "Take your time!" faded as she stepped inside and drew the door shut behind her.

Grateful for good neighbors like the Andersons, Kathryn backed out of the drive and headed toward the far end of Brighton Heath's boundary where the original homestead, which belonged to the Egan family, lay on the remaining four acres still in that name.

With the impending divorce, Nick had bequeathed everything to his offspring, changing his will just before leaving on his last news assignment. Since their separation had been one of mutual agreement and was not bitter, at least on the surface, he appointed Kathryn as a trustee of the boys' estate along with their longtime friend and attorney, Paul Radisson. As trustees, she and Radisson felt it was in the boys' best interest to develop the land, which more than quadrupled the value and resulted in a considerable fortune to invest for the minors' future.

It was hard to believe that five years ago all this was farmland and the house was a cold brick monster, isolated amid overgrown shrubs and trees. Nick's parents had bought the rundown place and worked it, but with their passing, the fields were rented for a pittance and the house became an oversized, under-modernized bachelor pad until she and Nick were married. Her mother was appalled at their living conditions, as Nick's career had not yet taken off and money to restore the house was not to be had.

Development had been a good decision, Kathryn thought as she turned into the large circle dubbed Egan Court. There the now-stately family home stood in all its Christmas splendor, as it might have appeared nearly two hundred years earlier when it had originally been built. Unlike its original state, however, it was insulated and boasted the latest indoor plumbing amenities as well as heating and air-conditioning. As one appraiser had put it, it was a two-hundred-year-old *new* home by the time Kathryn had finished restoring and remodeling it with some of the profits from the development.

Ordinarily she'd have taken time to appreciate the spacious yard, which was landscaped with its original ancient oak and walnut, as well as professionally restored beds and gardens. Egan Court had been featured in more than one of the house-and-garden magazines and now stood on the historical register as well. The restoration was a dream come true...a dream she and Nick had once shared. It saddened her that Nick had not survived to see it. No doubt, though, if he'd lived, he'd have spent more time reading about it than actually living in it.

Ah, no matter what was written about only good memories surviving a loved one's loss, the bitter still rose with the sweet from time to time. Kathryn pulled her minivan into the garage, an addition built on in the form of a carriage house. It was connected to the main manor by a long mud/utility room. The last of the items they intended to show were packed in boxes in the back of the car, but her assistant David and housekeeper Ruth Ann would have to get them out. She had to shower and dress in less than forty-five minutes!

In the mad rush into the house, Kathryn didn't take time to seek out her partner in this unconventional show scheme. Knowing David was efficiently devoting his time to the great room, she told her housekeeper to advise him of her arrival and the items in the car. While she hated delegating authority, there were some times when it was unavoidable, and, thanks to Jason, this was one of them.

The scent of the Cajun-blackened prime rib and its accompanying dishes being prepared by the caterers followed her as she scrambled up the servants' stairwell to the master suite. It reminded Kathryn that she'd missed lunch. Lying across the bed, à la David, was one of the Parisian designs she'd purchased for Mrs. Whitehall's fashion department at the Emporium. It was still in its protective plastic. Coordinating shoes, purse, and gloves, as well as a short matching velvet cape, were beside the dress, although Kathryn doubted she'd need the cape or purse inside the house. Maybe she'd display them on the coatrack in the hall, since with the rush she'd been in, she was in an overheated lather as it was.

Fortunately, she wasn't one to linger in the shower. Life did not allow her the luxury of using the porcelain pedestal tub with the slanted back in the light of the flickering electric sconces hanging on the walls. Instead she showered in a tiled cove adorned with stylish curtains to match those hanging over the shuttered window, making quick work of lavishing scented bath gel on her smooth skin. After drying with a thick coordinated towel, she rushed through her after-bath toilette and dried her hair recklessly, since she was going to wear her hair up anyway.

The dark green velvet of the dress fit her figure like a sheath. By the time Kathryn drew on the matching long silk gloves, she looked quite the princess, especially after she fastened a jeweled velvet comb in her hair to hold her upswept locks in place. With one last breathless look in the mirror, she dabbed on a touch of new perfume imported from Demonde of the Virgin Islands and hurried down the main staircase just as the walnut grandfather clock in the central hall struck six.

Six! But it should be seven! Kathryn stopped halfway in her descent and stared at the face of the elegantly carved Swiss timepiece in confusion; then it dawned on her that she'd been running on the schedule of the clock in the dash of her car. It had not yet been set back for daylight saving time. She was an hour *ahead* of schedule!

With a breath of mixed relief and exasperation over her unnecessary tizzy, she started downward again. Although thick oriental carpet on the grand staircase cushioned her steps, her descent drew the attention of the two well-dressed men conversing in the doorway of the great room. One was her assistant manager, David Marsh, and the other, Paul Radisson, her attorney and fellow trustee of the children's estate. The preparations must be completed or David would still be flitting about like a hyperactive hummingbird.

"David, you're a lifesaver!"

She stopped at the bottom of the steps to reseat her foot in the sequin-buckled high heels before she pulled a Cinderella act and left it in her wake. They were supposed to have been size 8, not 8 ½, but it was too late to do anything about it. They were designed to complement the rest of her ensemble.

Both men moved forward to steady her as she wrestled with the errant slipper, but David reached her first. "And you, Kathryn, are a work of art, not to mention an hour ahead of schedule. I take it you've solved the case of the prodigal son to the school's satisfaction?"

"For the time being, although this single working mother bit drives me batty at times. I'm only an hour early because I was rushing by a clock I hadn't set back yet."

"I'm willing to come to your rescue anytime," Paul Radisson spoke up. "Especially if you wear that dress! I'll wager that if the women coming tonight think they can look like you in it, you can't possibly have ordered enough of them."

"Only one of each style, dear." She patted his cheek. "It wouldn't do to have two ladies appear at the same function in the same dress." Aside from her, there would be models circulating among the guests for an additional peek at the new holiday apparel. "As for coming to my rescue, you already have by agreeing to act as my cohost. David and I will be frantically involved with sales if this works out the way we plan."

Paul had been Nick's best man at their wedding and for a while, he and his wife and she and Nick had socialized together. If only time could have stood still then—when they were all newlyweds, and, although struggling to make financial ends meet, so much in love. However, when Nick took the job of foreign correspondent and Paul graduated from law school to join his father's firm, the two couples drifted apart.

Upon her husband's violent death, Kathryn discovered that Paul had divorced his wife, although it didn't come as a complete shock. Word drifted down along her mother's grapevine that Paul had become something of a silver-tongued devil with the women in the elite social circles about D.C. He'd tried his charm on Kathryn, but to no avail…yet.

Even if he had truly had enough of his *freedom* as he claimed, she was not ready for a relationship beyond the one they had as friends and occasional escorts to thwart well-intentioned matchmakers like her mother and friends. Sometimes Kathryn wondered if she'd ever be receptive to another man.

She humored Paul with an absent smile as he made a gallant show of lifting her hand to his lips. While Nick had fallen short of her ideal of a husband, Paul was closer to it than any man she'd ever met. Maybe she was too picky, as her mother accused, but *once burned, twice shy*, as the saying goes. The most important requirement was that the man she chose had to be good father material for the boys, someone she and they could count on. They were the only men in her life that really mattered.

"Since I've a moment to catch my breath, I'd love a cup of the imported punch before the hoards arrive."

She withdrew her hand when he held it a moment longer than necessary. Yes, Paul would be perfect but for his discomfort around children.

"The alcohol-free English wassail," she requested with a thoughtful upturn of her lips. "I'm saving the spiced ciders for dinner."

"At your service, madam." Paul broke into a toothsome grin and winked. He'd given away excellent tickets to attend the symphony with his senior partners without complaint, just to be at her side. Kathryn couldn't help but appreciate his attentiveness and dedication.

"You're a dear for putting up with me."

"*Us*," David injected at her side as Paul retreated to the bar set up in the front parlor. "I was in such a dither, I asked *him* to help unpack the Venetian glassware."

Kathryn grinned at the *last resort* implication in David's voice. Like her, he was very particular and preferred doing things himself. Still, she couldn't imagine having to put the show together without her employer's nephew.

David joined the firm upon graduating from a European art school three years ago and seemed to soak up the knowledge she had to offer like a sponge. There was no doubt in her mind that the Whitehalls would leave the business to their only nephew, having no children of their own.

Then her assistant would become her boss, a prospect that didn't bother Kathryn in the least. The two of them operated on the same wavelength and with the same devotion to their trade. Too often they teased each other about being married to imports and not having time to seek personal relationships. David would no doubt make some young woman a delightful husband someday, if he ever left the store and import warehouses to find her.

Even then, the girl would likely need a four-hundred-year-old necklace displayed on her chest to catch his attention, just as a man would need some similar trappings to capture hers. They were a pot and kettle, if there ever was such a pair.

"Kathryn, you must see the table!" the young man went on in an enthusiastic burst. "The Canton is exquisite! Imagine finding it packed in a barrel of straw, untouched for two hundred years. I'll wager Jacob Witherby will purchase it at top price before the night's out."

"No way." Kathryn laughed, taking the crystal cup of wassail Paul handed her. "I know better than to risk good money against your instincts."

David's eyes twinkled with mischief and delight. "Why, Kathryn, I believe I'm flattered, considering my aunt thinks you the mistress extraordinaire of profitable intuition."

She stirred the steamy concoction with the cinnamon stick garnish, checking to be certain the mandatory apple slice was there in the bottom. Both came with the ready mix, which tasted as heavenly as if it were simmered on some ancient stone hearth.

Knowing her clientele, it was a certain sell to the Sharmas, whose parties were well known in the capital's diplomatic social circles. Kathryn sipped it slowly while inspecting the tastefully displayed items from all parts of the world. A showroom couldn't possibly display them to their best advantage, not like a real home.

Each piece looked as if it had been purchased for its particular space in the scheme of decor. From the authentic Queen Anne banquet tables, now set elaborately for twenty of the Emporium's most prestigious buyers on hand-embroidered Irish linen, to the carved rosewood occasional tables flanking richly upholstered furniture of Eastern design, there was an atmosphere of intimate elegance.

"David, it's perfect!" Kathryn beamed at her proud assistant. Before she could follow her comment through with an appreciative hug, the front bell rang.

Adrenaline pumped. "You start the music, I'll get the door," she ordered, feeling her face flush with anticipation.

Ruth Ann was too busy with the caterers in the kitchen to worry with admitting guests tonight, another reason Paul had been asked to cohost.

"It's probably the Whitehalls," she called over her

shoulder as she walked into the marbled hall, her heels clicking crisply on the polished surface not covered by Turkish area rugs. "After this, you can take over," she added, realizing she'd promptly assumed her cohost's assigned task.

Paul touched his heels together in mock salute. "Yes, mein madame! It's now my one goal in life to be your man."

Kathryn let the innuendo slide. It was hard to tell when Paul was serious or teasing, although David told her the man only fell back on the teasing angle to avoid her rejection and save his ego.

"Crazy!" she accused playfully, allowing Paul that out. Could she ever bring herself to take him seriously?

Brandishing a brilliant smile to wash away her doubt, she opened the front door. The wind had picked up, and the icy air rushed in to assault her back and shoulders, bared by the halter design of her gown. Instead of her employers, however, she found herself face-to-face with only one individual. He stood, shoulders hunched in a beige topcoat. His brown hair whipped about his face, while his breath fogged the air before a mouth frozen in a thin white line.

Somehow an incredulous "Nick!" escaped her tightening throat as Kathryn stared at the mature version of her son Jason. Were it not for the fact that her heart seemed to have stopped cold, the expectant whiskey-colored gaze fixed upon her would have negated the icy air rushing in and warmed her from head to toe as it always had.

But it couldn't be Nick. Kathryn felt her strength drain as quickly as the blood from her face, leaving a pinpricked trail of disbelief. *Nick was dead!* They'd sent home a few of his charred belongings, his body having been destroyed in the explosion beyond retrieval, much less identification. She buried them in his place. Pregnant with his second son, the one she hadn't told him about during the divorce negotiations, she'd wept at the small gravesite with guilt and grief until she could cry no more.

The memory reemerged with a terrible blow. Staggering a step backward, Kathryn blinked as if to erase this bizarre visitation of the ghost of Christmas past from her sight, but he remained there, studying her with an enigmatic gaze.

Suddenly he spoke, his voice as real as he appeared to be, the solemn line of his lips breaking in a poor attempt at humor.

"Hi, honey, I'm home."

SUMMIT by Karen Rispin
ISBN: 1-57673-402-1
Available now!

Julie threw back her head and let the mountain wind play with her hair. Kurt had actually agreed to come hiking with her. Maybe there was still a chance. Hope made her feet light, and she danced ahead of her fiancé, skipping from rock to rock. She hesitated, not wanting to get too far ahead. A rough gray boulder twenty feet high leaned over the path. It would be fun to wait on top.

Quickly she felt for handholds on the limestone. Perched like a pixie on top of the rock, she watched Kurt climb toward her. His stocky, muscular body looked good as he plodded deliberately upward. And yet, as she watched him, Julie felt her smile fade. Kurt was a good man. The kind of man her family expected her to marry. Mom and Dad had been so happy when she showed them her ring...

Julie's stomach tightened and she fought an urge to move away from Kurt, up the mountain toward the blue sky. She should be happy. In a month she'd be married to this wonderful Christian man. Instead her eyes suddenly stung with tears.

Kurt's head was down as he doggedly picked his way up the tumbled rocks. Just below her, he stopped.

His face red with exertion, Kurt scanned the path ahead of him with anxious eyes. "Julie!"

"I'm right here, Kurt."

His head snapped back as he looked up too quickly. He staggered backward, trying to catch his balance.

"Careful!" Julie's warning was too late. Kurt caught his heel on a stone and sat down hard.

Julie was already moving. She climbed quickly down the face of the boulder. In seconds she was at his side. She knelt and touched his arm. "I'm sorry; I didn't mean to startle you."

"Are you insane?" Kurt pushed her hand away and got to his feet in one sharp motion, glaring from her to the spot she'd been waiting.

Julie stepped back, her hand falling to her side. "It was an easy climb and not that high."

"You could have been killed. That's how much you care about our commitment? So little that you'd risk it all to perch on the top of a rock like some fool bird?" Kurt's fist chopped at the air. "One wrong move and you would have fallen! Been seriously injured, or even killed."

Julie reached out her hands to him. "Kurt, I wasn't in danger. This climb was easy, no more than a 5.7 level of difficulty." His eyes narrowed at her use of a climbing term, and she bit her lip. "I've been climbing at a much higher level for years, and I was careful. I made sure of each hold. I'm not foolish."

Kurt studied her, then shook his head. He reached out to take her hands. "I just don't want you hurt." His eyes held nothing but sincerity. "Julie, you are not a child anymore. You're an adult and we have a life to plan together. We should never have come here. The mountains are bad for you."

"No!" The word was forced out of her in a gasp of pain. In a flash of insight, Julie was sure of what she'd been fighting for months. She'd been trying to remake herself in a pattern that would please Kurt. But that was wrong. She couldn't do it anymore.

He tugged on her hands, drawing her into his arms. "Julie, sweetheart..." His mouth came down on hers. For a second she longed to stay there, safe in his arms. Safe as his wife. It would mean security, safety, the kind of life everyone wanted.

A vivid image of that life brought a rush of panic. It would mean many more endless months of working the job he'd found for her, then years of staying home with children in his stuffy suburban bungalow. Years of pretending to be another person.

Suddenly Kurt's arms and mouth seemed to suffocate her. She pulled away, twisting in his grip. Kurt released her so suddenly that she almost fell. Catching her balance, she backed away from him.

"What is wrong with you, Julie?" His eyes were

anxious, confused. "I thought you gave up all the childish, risky rock climbing stuff."

Julie kept backing up. Her throat was so tight with emotion it was hard to get the words out. "Guiding rock climbers is not childish. It isn't! I worked hard to get the qualifications to do that. It was a difficult and responsible job."

Kurt shook his head. "You agreed it was right to give all that up. A Christian wife shouldn't take those kinds of risks. She belongs with her husband in the home. We looked the verses up together, remember? Like the verses in Timothy that say a wife should be a keeper at home."

Julie clutched at the boulder to steady herself. "I tried, Kurt. I really did. I denied it, even to myself, but working in the bank has been stifling. God didn't make me to do that." She knew that was true. Knew it as sure as she knew her name. Conviction steadied her voice. "The mountains are good for me, not bad. I belong here, taking risks, teaching people the skills they need to be here. I feel God smiling at me when I climb. How can I stop being me?" She met his gaze, begging him with her eyes to understand. "Today when you said you'd come hike with me I was hoping..." She half reached out to him then dropped her hand helplessly.

Kurt shook his head. "Hoping what? Hoping I'd say it was fine? That my wife can go risk her life with strangers? Julie, that's crazy."

"Does it have to be?" Tears were streaming silently down her cheeks.

Kurt gave a little grunt of pain—she knew how it hurt him to see her cry—and moved toward her. Julie dodged him, but he caught her arm. "Julie, stop it. I love you. You're going to be my wife. You'll get over this."

Julie tried to shrug out of his grip. "How can I get over who I am? I can't marry you, Kurt. I can't be the person you want." Sadness swept over her. "No matter how much I wish I could."

Kurt's grip on her arm tightened. "No! Don't say that! You can't say that. You're mine, Julie Miller. We're getting married. The wedding is planned. Everyone would laugh at me."

Julie's vision blurred as her tears flowed more freely.

Kurt looked at her, then let go of her and turned his head away. "I've been afraid of this. I could sense you slipping away. Why, Julie? Why can't you grow up and settle down?"

"It's not a matter of growing up." She wanted to help him understand.

"Of course it is!" Kurt slammed one fist into the palm of his other hand. "Women are supposed to grow up and settle down. What I want from you is what the

Bible says a wife should be. Any man would want that. So what are you going to do, never get married at all?"

Julie stared at him, her throat tight and burning. Was he right? "I—I don't know." And she didn't. All she knew was that she couldn't take this conversation—or the feelings that were overwhelming her—one moment longer. She spun and ran away from Kurt. She ignored his voice calling after her as she sprinted hard up the mountain trail until she couldn't see through her tears. Stumbling to a stop, she leaned her forehead against the cool rock. She listened, but Kurt didn't come after her. Pain rolled over her, choking her, forcing itself out in deep sobs.

Kurt was right. She could never fit in the kind of marriage he'd described. His words rang in her ears, over and over. *"Any man would want that...Any man would want that..."*

She was going to be alone for the rest of her life.

She wanted to pray, to beg God for answers, but all that came out was one low, whispered sentence: "Father, help me."

After a long time her heart quieted. She looked up at the peak above her, gleaming against a deep blue sky. Its beauty sang to her of God's love. Julie stood and let the mountain wind cool her swollen eyes. If climbing was to be her world, then so be it. Maybe she couldn't honor God by being Kurt's wife, or by being anyone else's wife for that matter, but she could honor God by being an excellent climber and guide. She would focus on that with all her strength and accept the cost.

Men simply would not be a part of her future.

"I'm going to fall!" Ron's voice shook with fear. His elbows angled out like wings as he tried to hang on to the cliff face.

Dealing with her clients' fears was something Julie could handle. There were other things in her life that weren't so easy. She had thought she was getting better, but she'd had a jolt that morning that made her less sure. Julie shook her head and focused on Ron.

"Reach up. There's a big hold just above your right shoulder."

Ron didn't respond. He just hung there about forty feet above Julie's stance at the base of the cliff. His legs were shaking with fatigue from the unnatural crouched position he'd held since he started the climb.

"Come on, man. You can do this!" Murry called from just behind Julie. He and Ron played hockey together in a recreational league and talked about adventures. Deciding to try rock climbing, they'd found the Big Foot Outfitters ad in the yellow pages. As Big Foot's rock-climbing guide, Julie had ended up with the job of taking them on the day's climb.

Julie schooled her tone to be both firm and reassuring. "Stand up and get that hold, Ron. You can do it. If you fall, I've got you." He crouched slightly, then made a desperate lunge for the hold. Scrabbling, he managed to find footholds and keep his grip.

"All right!" Julie and Murry cheered.

Julie took up the slack on the rope. "You're past the hardest part of the climb, Ron." He kept moving upward in an uncoordinated scramble. He was obviously tired and was climbing badly, though the climb was not difficult. Just below the top his hands slipped. With a strangled bleat of terror, he fell.

Automatically, Julie's right hand moved down and outward, locking the rope in place. The stretch in the rope and the friction where it ran through the anchor at the top took some of Ron's weight. Even so, Julie sat hard in the harness to keep her feet on the ground. Her full concentration stayed on the climber.

"You can do this, Ron. Use your head and climb carefully." Julie nodded in satisfaction as Ron started moving again. "He's a brave guy," she commented to Murry. "That fall scared him badly. A lot of people would have quit."

"So what does that make you? Some kind of superwoman? When you put up the rope, you went up that cliff like it wasn't even there."

Julie cringed at the anger in Murry's voice. "This is

my work, okay?" Hearing her defensive tone of voice, she took a deep breath and focused on Ron as he hauled himself up the last few feet of the climb. No point in letting this guy get to her. No point in letting *any* guy get to her. Not again.

"Way to go, man!" Julie cheered as Ron reached the top. He whooped with exhilaration as he slapped the tree at the top of the pitch.

Julie laughed. "Now, put your feet on the rock and walk backward. I'll let you down."

"People who do this are crazy," Ron called as he complied.

"Isn't it the best?" Julie couldn't hold back her enthusiasm. She loved everything about climbing: the height; the roughness and beauty of the rock itself; the isolated wild places where she worked; the strength, grace, and discipline it took to learn a new face; and the self-reliance it demanded. Most of all, she loved the way the wild country spoke to her of God. His power and awesome beauty were evident everywhere in the mountains.

By the time Ron reached the ground his grin was huge. He and Murry whooped and gave each other high fives.

Julie watched them with a half smile on her face. It would be nice if she could feel that same exhilaration, that sense of victory with her problem, but she had no idea how to do that, or even if it could be done.

She shook her head. It was much better to concentrate on enjoying the moment at hand. She flipped her long dark braid over her shoulder and pulled out candy bars for the celebration, handing them to the two men. "So, do you guys want to climb here again to consolidate the things you've learned or shall we move to another climb?"

"I want to try this climb without the Ukrainian dance style." Ron grinned as he stood and stretched.

Watching him, Julie's mouth tightened. When Ron had gotten out of his car that morning, she'd thought for a stunned second that he was Kurt. She'd realized almost instantly that the resemblance was only superficial. As the morning went on, she'd almost been able to put it out of her mind. But the way he'd moved just now as he stood and stretched was so painfully familiar. . . .

Ron hesitated. "Hey, don't look at me like that. If you want us to move on, that's fine with me."

"Sorry, I was thinking about something else." Julie handed him the end of the rope. "See if you can tie yourself in."

She watched as Ron climbed again, this time with more confidence. As she lowered Ron down the face, Murry nodded at her. "Okay, I'll try again too."

Julie was checking Murry's knot when the sound

of approaching footsteps turned their heads.

"There you are, Julie."

She looked up in surprise. Her boss's smooth voice couldn't be mistaken. "Hi, Brent." She watched him warily. A tireless self-promoter in his late thirties, Brent radiated good will as he introduced himself to Ron and Murry as the owner of Big Foot Outfitters.

"I just wanted to make sure Julie was treating you right." Brent thumped Julie on the back. He looked through the screen of trees at the base of the slabs and motioned expansively. "David, come here. I want you to meet these people."

It was only then that Julie realized another man had come with Brent. Maybe another climber to join her party? Still, it was odd that Brent would bring the person himself. She looked at Ron and Murry, wondering if they'd mind, then back at the newcomer. She hesitated as the man's eyes met hers. Confidence and calm. That's what she saw in that level gray gaze. He was lean and wiry, more than six feet tall with curly dark hair.

"David, I want you to meet Julie, and Ron and Murry, who are climbing with her."

"It's a pleasure." David's English accent surprised Julie as he held out his hand. She realized she'd been staring and reached to shake his hand. It was unexpectedly hard with calluses. She glanced down and saw that the back of his hand was marked with scars and scrapes:

a climber's hand. His sinewy forearm was ridged with muscle. This was no new climber.

Julie glanced at Brent in puzzlement as David shook hands with her climbers. Brent caught Julie's curious look and came to stand beside her.

"He's Big Foot's new climbing guide," he explained in a quiet aside to Julie. "He just got in this morning. I was showing him around and thought we'd stop to meet you."

Julie had been watching David, but her attention snapped back to Brent.

"You hired a full-time climbing guide? Why?" She was supposed to be Big Foot's guide. "Is this guy internationally certified as a climbing guide?"

"He is. Remember when I went to England last summer? David Hales was my guide, and I told him he had a job here if he ever came over." Brent shrugged. "Well, he came. He'll be here until mid-September."

"You must have been doing paperwork for months to get work permits and stuff. How come you never said anything?"

Brent frowned. "Don't get in my face, Julie. You're good with clients, but replacing you wouldn't be hard. David is a world-class climber and those aren't thick on the ground. He's supposed to be a good teacher. You should be glad for the chance to work with him occasionally."

Occasionally! She was going to lose work. She blinked and tried to focus on what Brent was saying.

"Besides, you should be happy to have him around. His nickname is the Vicar."

"What is that supposed to mean?"

Brent didn't answer because David and the other two had quit talking. Julie watched Brent turn on the charm full bore for his clients. "So, what do you think of climbing now that you've tried it?"

Both men responded enthusiastically to Brent and in a few seconds were talking animatedly about their experience.

Julie found David looking at her.

"Your name is Julie; is that right?"

She nodded.

"I'm looking forward to working with you. I'm sure you can teach me a few things about climbing around here."

Brent looked over and laughed. "You'll teach her a few things, more like. Julie, I'll need you tomorrow after all. I'll send someone to get you at 6:30 A.M. Come on, David, let's go. Julie has some climbers here who want to get on the rock."

David hesitated, his eyes still on Julie, but Brent motioned impatiently. Julie watched them walk off, two long, lean men striding together.

Julie set her jaw. It was no use admitting that the

Englishman was attractive. There was no room for men in her life. Hadn't she learned that lesson already? Especially some British climbing star who was going to completely mess up her plans. And her life.